Tim Scul...

Breakthrough
GHOST PHOTOGRAPHY
of
HAUNTED HISTORIC COLONIAL
WILLIAMSBURG, VIRGINIA

PART II

Schiffer
Publishing Ltd

4880 Lower Valley Road • Atglen, PA 19310

Other Schiffer Books by the Author:

Haunted Historic Colonial Williamsburg Virginia: With Breakthrough Ghost Photography.
ISBN: 978-0-7643-5060-3

Other Schiffer Books on Related Subjects:

Dead Whispers: Ghostly EVPs. A. E. Angel
ISBN: 978-0-7643-4236-3

EVP: Electronic Voice Phenomenon: Massachusetts Ghostly Voices.
Mike Markowicz
ISBN: 978-0-7643-3359-0

Cover design by Molly Shields

Type set in Tw Cen MT/Times New Roman

ISBN: 978-0-7643-5572-1
Printed in China

Published by Schiffer Publishing, Ltd.
4880 Lower Valley Road
Atglen, PA 19310
Phone: (610) 593-1777; Fax: (610) 593-2002
E-mail: Info@schifferbooks.com
Web: www.schifferbooks.com

For our complete selection of fine books on this and related subjects, please visit our website at www.schifferbooks.com. You may also write for a free catalog.

Schiffer Publishing's titles are available at special discounts for bulk purchases for sales promotions or premiums. Special editions, including personalized covers, corporate imprints, and excerpts, can be created in large quantities for special needs. For more information, contact the publisher.

We are always looking for people to write books on new and related subjects. If you have an idea for a book, please contact us at proposals@schifferbooks.com.

Thanks to my wife and family for putting up with all of my late-night jaunts into Colonial Williamsburg. Thanks to author P. A. Spade for all your help and support.

Thanks also to former Colonial Williamsburg security officer Chuck Rayle and to former Colonial Williamsburg interpreter Tom Williams for their stories and insights.

TO MY READERS

This book is for all of those individuals who have to see something before they believe it. Williamsburg has more eighteenth-century buildings (eighty-eight) than any other place in America—with at least one or more ghostly apparitions at each of them—hence my contention that it is America's most haunted place. The ghosts are even at the buildings and homes that are not original; in fact, every building on the Duke of Gloucester Street, dubbed "the most historical avenue in all America" by Franklin D. Roosevelt, has one or more apparitions over it. I would like to hail it as "the most haunted avenue in all America."

This book is a look into a world we cannot see with the naked eye. The advanced electronics of the digital camera have become the eyes through which we can see evidence of the paranormal! Most ghosts, apparitions, phantoms, wraiths, or whatever you choose to call them, have an appearance like nothing you have ever imagined—are you ready for proof of an alternate realty?

• • • • •

Though you do not need to read or view my first book to understand and enjoy Part II, your enjoyment and learning would benefit from it. *Haunted Historic Colonial Williamsburg, Virginia: with Breakthrough Ghost Photography.* (ISBN: 978-0-7643-5060-3, www.schifferbooks.com, www.facebook.com/timscullionauthor)

"WHERE ARE THE DEAD? ARE THEY STILL AMONGST US, POSSESSED OF THAT UNDEFINED, MYSTERIOUS EXISTENCE WHICH THE ANCIENT WORLD ATTRIBUTES TO THE GHOSTS OF THE DEPARTED?"

—Charles Lindley Wood (1839–1934)
Lord Halifax's Ghost Book: A Collection of True Stories, first published in 1936

The dead are within the pages of this book, waiting for you to discover this undefined paradigm. Perhaps even Lord Halifax himself exists in this netherworld, casting out hints of his presence to those who are unaware. Now you will learn what becomes of those caught between this world and the next—and what they really look like . . .

—Tim Scullion

—— CONTENTS ——

ACKNOWLEDGMENTS

I worked for several years as a tour guide in Colonial Williamsburg, and I had to learn a lot of facts and dates, as well as the culture of both the eighteenth-century colonists and the Native Americans. I would like to gratefully acknowledge the historians, archeologists, and researchers of Colonial Williamsburg as my source for the background information for each home or building from Colonial Williamsburg shown in this book. I thought that it was important to give you some background history about the house or building; if you would like to read further check out Colonial Williamsburg's websites (start with www.history.org/) or their publications. From time to time, due to the discovery of new archeological evidence or documents, Colonial Williamsburg will revise their interpretation of buildings, eighteenth-century life, and history. This book was meticulously researched for accuracy through Colonial Williamsburg's historical reports, its official guide, and its archeological reports. Should any information in this book become outdated through new discoveries, please notify the author so that appropriate changes can be made.

INTRODUCTION

The photos you are about to view are an amazing look into an alternate reality. I continue to learn, and I continue to be amazed by what I discover in this netherworld that most people do not want to admit exists. Unintentionally, my journey for this book begins in the Southwest, where I discovered things when I was not even looking for them; but more about that later. If you recall from my first book (Part I), I too was a self-described skeptic about the existence of ghosts—I had never experienced any type of paranormal activity in my life. When I began to take the photos, I began to look for a rational explanation for the existence of these creatures. I found the hypothesis of physicist Janusz Slawinski intriguing: Based on the two scientific facts that all living creatures give off photons of light, and that when a living organism dies it emits a "death flash" of electromagnetivity that can be up to a thousand times stronger than the standing rate of emission, he concluded that our mind is an *electromagnetic conscious self* that survives the death of the physical body.[1] As I processed that I wondered why our physical brain would have or even need this; wouldn't this center of awareness or consciousness exist somewhere within the structures of the human brain? I had to learn more, and that's when I discovered the work of Dr. Johnjoe McFadden.

To answer the above question, *no*, researchers can find no region or structure in the human brain that houses the consciousness. Rene Decartes, in his fundamental statement of existence, wrote, "I think, therefore I am"; but where and what is the "I"? According to Dr. McFadden, the brain's central processing unit (CPU) that binds together all of the thousands of nerve signals that come in at one time is an *electromagnetic field*. Without this binding field that makes sense of everything and how it relates to the "I," all of this information would be like pieces of a jigsaw puzzle scattered on a table. This electromagnetic field binds all of the nerve signals (from all of the senses) together to produce a complete picture, and creates a synchronous firing of neurons to induce a physical reaction, if necessary.[2] Of course, this is a simplified explanation for what our consciousness is, but the idea is that what makes us conscious, living, breathing beings is something separate from the human body: The "I" is an electromagnetic ghost! Can you imagine what this means for mental illness? Would you treat the physical brain, or the electromagnetic soul? What are the implications for creating artificial intelligence? On the one hand, things just got a lot more complicated, but on the other, Professor McFadden may have provided a rational explanation for the photos in this book.

I have made new discoveries about apparitions, which I am excited to relate to you so that you can form your own conclusions and hypothesis about the paranormal. I have included a second look at Williamsburg's most haunted dwelling, the Peyton Randolph House—from the back and the side. I have a plethora of new photos, stories, and anomalies in this book, and an amazing personal experience of the paranormal at my very own house, which is right on the historic route that five different armies traveled: the English army under Lord Cornwallis, the Continental (American) army under the command of George Washington, the French army (marching with Washington) under General Rochambeau, the retreating Confederate army under General Johnston, and the Union army under George McClellan.

This book and my first one, more than anything, have been a personal odyssey to discover the answer to the age-old question: Is there life after death? Have people made up stories for thousands of years just to entertain each other, or was it a bona fide experience? I believe the photographs answer that question in a way that I never imagined. Had you come to me a few years before and told me that this is what I would be doing, I would have told you that you were crazy! Now I have discovered that ghosts are everywhere; a house doesn't have to be historic or really old to have one or more ghosts. I have found them in the desert, in cornfields, in the parking lots of shopping centers, in new houses, even in the water.

Come with me on Part II of my journey into the unknown to look at the faces of those who choose to stay behind, for whatever reason, and who try to make their presence known to those still in the world they once inhabited.

Photo Editing—for Ones Who Need It

If you recall, I began this odyssey as a skeptic, and I was not fully convinced of the paranormal until I had several hundred photos of something that I still do not fully understand. I think that it's also a defense mechanism not to believe in what we cannot comprehend, which is where a lot of skeptics are coming from. But when you look at the whole gamut of human understanding, you will discover that although we have come a long way, there are still more

questions than answers. So I understand where some people are coming from when they express disbelief at some of the photos I've taken. They do not know my character, and they immediately assert that the photos in this book and my first book were contrived in Photoshop, and so I want to address that issue from the start. Since you do not know me personally, anything that I write about myself would be called into question, and besides, I am not the type of person to write about myself that way. I am of the mind that you can only address a person's meddle through the eyes of other people, otherwise you are just engaging in self-aggrandizement.

So let's discuss the photographs: In my first book, I addressed that issue in what I thought was sufficient manner, but it appears I must go a bit further. Many of the photos require no adjustments and are posted as they appeared in my camera—no modifications in any kind of computer program, including the software that came with my cameras or with Photoshop. In fact, I have set aside these photos both on a camera chip and in a folder that I hope to one day submit to a qualified photographic expert to verify that they have not been modified in any way. I wanted to show first off two of these photos, emphasizing again that they have not been altered in any way! Later on in this book I will show them again with an explanation into the circumstances and the surroundings for each photo. I chose these two photos because of the bizarre appearance of each "ghost"—or whatever you choose to call them, and to make the comment that I would have never guessed that they looked like this. But then again, I'm forced to wonder if they have the ability to create holograms of whatever they choose—much the way film producers create the likeness of creatures from the depths of their imagination, and not just the likeness of their former selves.

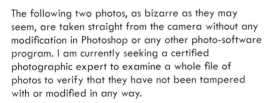

The following two photos, as bizarre as they may seem, are taken straight from the camera without any modification in Photoshop or any other photo-software program. I am currently seeking a certified photographic expert to examine a whole file of photos to verify that they have not been tampered with or modified in any way.

Now I would like to address photos that do need editing, and what I do to them. In Chapter 28 of my first book, *I explained the photo-editing process to be as transparent as possible.* I showed what the photo looked like in the beginning, and then showed the sequence of photos from start to finish explaining the process to get a clearer, more definable photo. I showed an apparition that appeared in two windowpanes of a larger window, with a rather elongated face, and explained that I zoomed in on the windowpanes, cropped the photo, and then enlarged it (the photo was only about a half-inch wide in the beginning). I then turned up the contrast a bit so that you could see the facial details better, and then finally I

removed the grain or pixilations from the photo so that the face would appear clear. These are some of the same techniques used by law enforcement to be able to hone in on facial details when analyzing videos taken of a crime scene or accident, and they are used in the court system as valid proof. Satellite imagery will also crop, enlarge, and remove the grain or pixilations (although they may not have to turn up the contrast because the images were taken during daylight), and these photographs are perfectly acceptable to the public and even law enforcement. The whole idea is not to alter the photo; just make what's there clearer so that the facial detail can be seen and perhaps the individual identified. I hold that these photos should likewise hold up in the court of public opinion.

When my first book was released, a man reviewed it after obtaining a free copy from my publisher, and he began to post his commentary on as many sites as he could find,

Step 1: Crop the original photo (in this case) to show an elongated face in both windowpanes.

Step 2: Enlarge the photo from one-half inch to two inches. Steps 3 and 4: Turn up the contrast and take the grain out of the photo.

misleading people about the editing process and denigrating the whole book. So to make sure you understand the process of the photos (only when needed), I want to make clear that the whole face of the apparition in the **above** photo occupies two windowpanes, and that the top window pane has the top of the ghost's head, the lower pane has the rest of the head. Nowhere do I state or infer that the image in the top windowpane becomes the image in the bottom—they are part of the same face! So hopefully you will see and comprehend that the photos are edited to make what's already there more visible and definable—and not to alter the features or create something that wasn't there.

One thing that I have done that helps to convince people of the existence of ghosts is to create and lead a ghost tour in Colonial Williamsburg that shows the photos that I have taken at each house or building (on a large-screen computer notebook). I also point out which windows the apparitions appeared in, and encourage those on the tour to take their own photos with their cell phone cameras (or whatever they have). Likewise, I let them know that they need to enlarge each photo, and perhaps turn up the contrast in order to see if they were successful in capturing the paranormal digitally. Many (but not all) have been delighted to find that they too were successful in capturing a wraith, even though they do not have the advanced camera technology that I use. I think that this helps validate the work that I've done in this book and my first book. I can guide people to capture ghosts on their own personal cameras, and if enough people do this, the paranormal will not be such an anomaly!

My goals are to help create a camera with better technology, so that these adjustments can be done on the camera. I am also looking into other ways to create better images, and hope to work with one of the major camera manufacturers to help create a camera that uses other means to enhance images. I believe that one day, whether it's myself or someone else, we will be able to see clearly into this alternate reality with technology so advanced it removes any doubts about the existence of the paranormal. But for now, let's look at the haunting faces in Colonial Williamsburg and then branch out into the surrounding areas!

Terms from Part I

There are a few esoteric terms that I coined in Part I that may be useful for you to know/ remember that I will be using in Part II; refer back to Part I for larger photos that show more detail. (Keep in mind that the first three are interchangeable—they can shape-shift in a matter of seconds into one of the other types.)

Red Super Cell—a kind of red, oval-shaped apparition usually found floating near or over top of a house or building. They can be as large as about seven feet (two meters) or as small as a softball. They always have a "V" marking pointing to the front side.

Spherical Torch—a sphere-shaped apparition with a torch-like light over top of it. They are usually alone, but can occasionally be seen in a pair; if another is present they usually lean to one side as if submissive. Colors seem to stay towards the yellow to red end of the visible light spectrum.

Geo-light—(short for geometrically-shaped light) an apparition made up of elaborately shaped light formations of various colors that resemble a work of modern art.

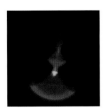

Fountain Shape—possibly a different version of the spherical torch, usually seem in cold weather. Colors seem to stay towards the green and blue end of the visible light spectrum.

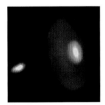

Yellow Umbrella—a small, yellow apparition that resembles an umbrella laying open on its side. There are slight variations on the shape and colors, but there is always a red super cell nearby—perhaps part of the same apparition. Since this part is usually resting on the house or building and the red super cell can be seen floating farther away, could this be the sensory gathering part of the apparition?

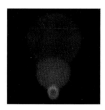

Red Balloon—a small, red apparition that looks like a single or double red balloon and always appears near a spherical torch. Like the yellow umbrella, since this part is usually resting on the house or building and the spherical torch can be seen floating farther away, could this be the sensory gathering part of the apparition?

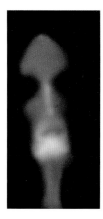

Classic White—an apparition that may have all or some facial features (eyes, nose, mouth), has an all-white appearance and resembles a classic Halloween-type ghost. It does not have enough distinguishing features to be identified as a specific person.

THE COKE-GARRETT HOUSE SHAPESHIFTER

When Is a "Lens Flare" Not a Lens Flare?
When It Moves and Shapeshifts!

Ghosts come in several different forms, two of which people are somewhat comfortable with and one that does not fit within their paradigm of what a ghost should look like—so they reject it. I have found that readers are comfortable with the ghosts that look like classic Halloween ghosts (which I call classic whites); they are comfortable with the ghosts that have definable human faces and resemble their former selves, but many reject the idea that the colored-light formations with different geometric shapes—what I call geo-lights—are nothing more than lens flares.

When is a lens flare not a lens flare? When it moves—and the camera is stationary on a tripod! When it shapeshifts from one photo to the next—and the photos are taken in quick succession. So what I would like to do is address this and several other issues that you may have with the photographs in this book so that you are comfortable with their veracity.

Electromagnetic Consciousness . . . or Lens Flare?

Before we get back to the Coke-Garrett House and the shapeshifter, let's clarify the word *lens flare* and differentiate it from the apparitions that I have photographed. How? By looking at the different patterns and shapes of the lens flares in other people's photographs and in video from commercials, television, and movies via an Internet search, and then comparing them to the apparitions in this book, hopefully you will be able to differentiate between the two. What I do know is that the apparitions I have photographed have a consistent pattern of geometric shapes and colors—does a lens flare have that kind of consistency, or is it just random? Lens flare, according to the writers at *Popular Photography*, is defined as follows:

> Lens flare is caused when light enters the lens at such an angle that the light rays do not completely flow through the lens but instead are reflected back and forth between lens elements. The sunspots created typically show the shape of the diaphragm (aperture blades) the camera was using at the time the photo was created.

If you recall from the Part I collection, according to scientific research, all living organisms give off photons (of light). Upon the death of an organism, the radiation of light can be up to 1,000 times greater than the mean emission. This is called a "deathflash," and it is independent of the cause of death. These statements have been proven by scientific research and have given rise to a hypothesis put forth by physicist Janusz Slawinsky that we have an electromagnetic consciousness and that this "necrotic radiation" is able to survive the death of the physical body.

What does it all mean? It's a scientific explanation for life with and without a physical body (ghosts!), and it also is an explanation for these low-level light formations that show up in photographs. The difference between a lens flare and the light formations that I have captured is that the latter has specific patterns of shapes and colors that show up on a consistent basis. The vast majority of photos with lens flare that you can look up on the Internet have a different, random pattern from the electromagnetic apparitions I have photographed—although there are a few that are incorrectly labeled as "lens flare" or more appropriately given the moniker "ghosting."

Although I maintain that these light apparitions are conscious, living beings and not lens flares, I wanted to address one more point about this: I believe that the apparitions in the chain react much like a lens flare when you move the camera around—at times stretching and at others compressing the shapes in the apparition chain, depending on the angle of the camera. I believe that's because these creatures are so large—I've photographed some that must be more than ninety-eight feet (thirty meters) in circumference! But the same types of apparitions show up in the same order every time, indicating that it is not showing the shape of the diaphragm. I believe that these are the electromagnetic "hot spots" within the creature, emitting photons of light as the creature thinks and as such reacts to the lens of a camera much like a lens flare—only with a consistent pattern of shapes and colors possibly indicating an intelligent being. Now just wait—notice that I said *possibly*, and then please wait for further explanation before you cast judgment . . .

The reason that I suggest an "intelligent being" is threefold: Movement and shapeshifting are the two visual indicators. If I take a photo of a house, building, or place (such as the Bruton Parish Church on the next page), with the constant of the camera sitting on a tripod in the same place, a lens flare should stay the same each time. But if these light anomalies move, and change shape with all other things as constant, then they cannot be a lens flare. Finally, when I have taken several psychics with me, I always ask them to point where they sense the location of the ghost. Invariably, when I take the photograph, the source of conscious thought that they detected is the geo-light apparition. Now let me show you a series of photos of the Coke-Garrett House, demonstrating movement and shapeshifting, and then you can make your own judgment call based on what you see! (Please note that I will post the background of the house and its paranormal history with the photos, because I'm trying to prove the point that the images you are seeing are not lens flares!)

The Coke-Garrett House, where the President of Colonial Williamsburg usually resides, is a very large, beautiful colonial house that is right next to the jail. In 1755, John Coke, a successful goldsmith and tavern keeper and owner of three lots, bought two more to the west (next to the jail)—evidently with a house already built on them, to consolidate the property you see today. The section that you see to the left predates 1755; however, the central, two-story portion was not added until 1837, and the section on the right dates sometime after that. From the Coke family the house changed hands quite a few times among businessmen of Williamsburg, including a baker, silversmith, gaoler (jailer), ordinary keeper (bed and breakfast), barber, constable, burgess, perukemaker (wigmaker), and carpenter, until the Garrett family purchased it. It remained in their hands until it was purchased by the Colonial Williamsburg Foundation, and became the residence of its president.

The Coke-Garrett House played an important role in the bloody battle of Williamsburg: It was a Confederate hospital during the conflict; shattered arms and legs from wounded soldiers were cut off and thrown into "amputation pits," and nearby, the dead were buried in mass graves. Amongst all of this carnage, at least one Confederate soldier has stayed behind to relive his final moments throughout time: He was fatally shot trying to rescue a wounded soldier from his regiment. Although mortally wounded, he managed to drag both himself and the fellow soldier back to the Coke-Garrett House. The man he saved lived, but he died and has been seen lying in the yard, still in a Confederate uniform with a bloody mark at the point the Union bullet pierced it. A number of witnesses have seen him one second on the ground groaning in pain, and then a moment later he has disappeared from sight. It makes you wonder why these apparitions seem to be locked into reliving the tragic moments that ended their lives over and over throughout time; will this troubled soul ever find peace?

An apparition (possibly of the Confederate soldier mentioned in the previous story?) stays to the far left of the property near an ancient tree. One evening, on the night of the October full moon, I decided to take a photograph of just that portion of the property. I realize that most people get excited when they see photographs of real faces, but I got excited by what I saw at this house: I observed, through a sequence of photographs, an apparition go through a metamorphosis of shape and color that was absolutely amazing—amplifying the proof that these apparitions are not just lens flares, but real electromagnetic consciences—ghosts! Keep in mind that I took this sequence of photos on a tripod, so the camera was not

These four photographs of the Bruton Parish Church show the shape-shifting ability of the apparitions as well as movement. All three were taken from almost identical spots on different nights with the same camera and the same lens. Lens flairs? I don't think so . . .

moving, and the photos were taken in quick succession, with barely a millisecond between takes. In addition to shape and color, the apparition changed from a compact shape of maybe several feet across (about one meter) to a gigantic apparition that rendered my wide-angle lens incapable of capturing the whole thing. It leaves the imagination taking flight with the idea that these creatures are capable of making themselves into any size, color, and shape of light that they want. Up until now shapeshifting was something for science fiction film, television, or prose; now you have the reality of limitless possibilities with creatures that were probably once human. Now take a look at the photographic evidence from the Coke-Garrett House that shows an even wider range of appearance possibilities for these apparitions. What do you think? Are the possibilities endless?

Finally, in an addendum to the shapeshifting apparition at the tree, I finally (after two years) was able to capture a face that showed up in a softball-sized orb of white light at the base of this very same tree; so the question that I have for myself and you: Is this the face of the wounded Confederate soldier who lost his life trying to save his friend and who died on the lawn of this house in front of the ancient tree?

The Coke-Garrett House has only one red super cell that hangs over the house, but the old tree in the front left side of the yard (out of sight) will be the focus of the shape-shifting apparition.

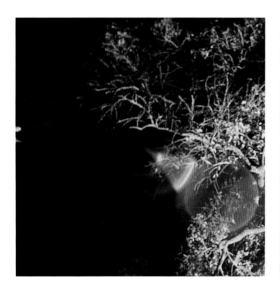

Here is the tree in front of the Coke-Garrett with the apparition that undergoes a major change in appearance—amazing example of shape-shifting happening in this sequence within seconds!

In this second photo, cropped around the moving apparition, it moves away from the first tree, morphing into several separate shapes.

The third photo at the Coke-Garrett House shows the apparition morphing into a gigantic hexagon-shaped apparition along with several smaller hexagons.

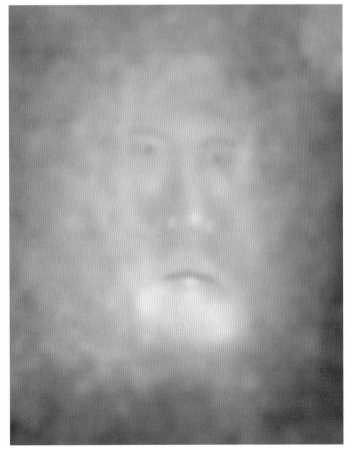

A long time after this sequence of photos was taken, I captured a softball-sized orb at the foot of the tree. When I zoomed in on it, I found this face. Could this be the Confederate soldier who died in the front yard trying to save his friend?

THE CHARLTON COFFEE HOUSE AND THE ANTHONY HAY CABINET SHOP

Does Running Water Attract, If Not Empower, Ghosts?

The Charlton Coffee House

Negative ions equal a positive sense of well-being. It doesn't make sense—especially for ghost hunters. Why is that, you say? Well it seems that many people seem to feel that ghosts feed off of negative energy, which I guess in essence is summed up as undesirable or depressed feelings of the living people that occupy the same house. Does that mean that negative feelings are the result of exposure to positive ions? I can't answer that question right now, because the research is just not there. Before I continue, let me tell you how I arrived at this conundrum.

I don't normally watch the plethora of paranormal shows on television, but one evening I was channel surfing, and I came across one of them long enough to hear the statement that ghosts are attracted to homes that are by or built over running water. I had never heard that statement made before, so I continued to watch. It was said that running water creates energy and gives off negative ions, and that supposedly attracts ghosts. So I immediately tried to find out if this was hearsay or if there was scientific proof to back what was said.

In my research, the first thing that I came across was "evidence" pushed by the manufacturers of negative ion generators—perhaps a little skewed? Then I found one website touting the benefits of negative ions,

saying that they acted like antidepressants—and yet another study found that sea spray gives off positively charged particles. So I'm thinking if negative ions are good and conversely positive ions are bad—why does everyone want to go to the beach?

Here's more conflicting information: One PhD who studies the brain says that negative ions increase the flow of oxygen to the brain, which increases alertness, but then another doctor says that negative ions have a calming effect that results in the release of serotonin, which helps us to sleep and reach REM (a deeper stage of sleep characterized by rapid eye movement) faster. So which is it, increased alertness or calming effect to go to sleep? Finally, I found a *meta-analysis* (a study that takes the results of all other studies on a certain subject, during a certain time period, to try to look for a consensus of results) that summed it up this way: The quality of many studies is low and inconsistent, resulting in this conclusion: ". . . there is no scientific basis for concluding that air ions have a beneficial or adverse effect on measures of anxiety, mood, relaxation/sleep, and personal comfort in the range of exposures reviewed." (Perez, Alexander, and Bailey; 2013).

So with the negative ion theory shot down, I decided to photograph two buildings—one that is next to a running stream (the Charlton Coffee House), and one that is built over a running stream (the Cabinet Makers Shop) to see if there was any plausibility to this theory.

My first stop was the Charlton, and I did find quite a few faces willing to show themselves in the windows. For such a small building, it was more than average, but then the Slave Quarters (from the first book) seemed to have more activity, and yet it was much smaller than the coffee house and without running water flowing next to it. So it's not definitive proof, but I did run across a problem; I have to give you some background on the Charlton Coffee House for you to understand.

As is so often the case, colonists in Virginia tried to create home away from home; in other words they tried to recreate all of the things that they had in England here in America. Coffee houses appeared in England during the mid-seventeenth century (1600s), and they became popular not only for their beverages— coffee, tea, and chocolate—but also as a gathering place to discuss news, business, politics, and even sedition. This would lead the English government to first license (1663) and later try to suppress (1675) coffee houses— so is it any wonder that the Charlton Coffee House may have been the breeding ground for the movement to independence?

So where would the ideal place to set up a coffee house be here in America? Right next to the Capitol, where the legislators could convene after a formal session for an informal one. So in the early 1760s, a young immigrant named Richard Charlton, wanting a bit of the old country in his new country, converted the building (which was a store) that sat next to the Capitol into a coffee house. Charlton was a wigmaker, and during the times that the legislators were not in session, he would also make wigs in the back rooms. Legislative sessions, called "publick times," took place in April and October, so Charlton would wash and restyle wigs for patrons and other Williamsburg residents during slack periods. During its ten-year run, the Charlton served

the likes of Washington, Jefferson, and even the royal governor of Virginia, Francis Fauquier. You see, that in order for the upper classes to patronize this establishment, it would have to have fitting accommodations. So one room, the "southeast room" (on the Capitol side), had plastered walls covered in wallpaper, with better furniture, better pictures on the walls, and more than likely a fine carpet. Evidently this was an alternative to the Raleigh Tavern for the burgesses—a place where they could engage in scholarly debate without the effects of alcohol (although Charlton would eventually serve alcohol, too). By contrast, the "southwest room" had pine boards on the walls, a simple fireplace, and a bar where the drinks were served—simple surroundings for the common man. According to archeological digs on the site, the discovery of more than 30,000 animal bones in the trash pit indicates that this coffee house was also a restaurant.

Charlton married a dressmaker, and so it is very likely that she based her business out of this building, too. The couple, who would remain childless, lived in the rather cramped second-floor area (which is really not a full second story, but more like an attic). Charlton's success in the 1760s must have, for some unknown reason, changed to misfortune by 1771: He moved to a less expensive backstreet house in the city and partnered with another man to continue his livelihood of making wigs. By 1776, that business failed and he would die just three years later. Another owner took over the coffee house, but when Governor Thomas Jefferson moved the capital from Williamsburg to Richmond in 1779, the site would **never again be used as a coffee house that catered to Virginia's elite**. By the 1880s, the building was just a shadow of its former self, tattered and dilapidated, and hardly worth the patronage of anyone, let alone the founding fathers that once darkened its doorstep.

The Armistead family owned the property in the 1880s, and they decided to raze the original structure and build a new "Victorian"-style home on the original foundation of the coffee house and with some of the structural materials incorporated into the new home. When the last of that branch of the Armistead family died in the 1990s, Colonial Williamsburg obtained the property and moved the two-story home to another site in Williamsburg—because the Victorian home was decidedly out of place in their vision to recreate an authentic eighteenth-century setting. Then they received a five-million-dollar grant to reconstruct the Charlton Coffee House. (Yes, I think that price tag sounds excessive for this building, regardless of using eighteenth-century methods to build it.)

Here is the Charlton Coffee House, a rather small, unassuming place that served the likes of Washington, Jefferson, and Henry, as well as the royal governor of Virginia.

I photographed and documented the Armistead House that was moved later on in this book for the unusual apparitions that I captured there, but that leaves me with this conundrum: Did the spirits of the Armistead family move with their Victorian house to the new address, or am I looking at them inside the coffee house? Whose apparitions occupy the home at its new address—the Armisteads, or the people who lived, worked, or owned the property before the house was moved there? I've stated before that ghosts will occupy a rebuilt building—so is it the ground that they are attached to? Conversely, I've heard that ghosts will haunt or possess objects, such as dolls, or even cars. So the faces in the windows of the rebuilt coffee house could be Armistead, Charlton, or the people who lived and/or worked there before or after its stint as the first coffee house at the Capitol of the largest English colony in America.

So the conventional theory is that running water can amplify the paranormal activity; I, however, cannot state that this home, according to the photographic results, has any more ghosts than some of the others that do not have running water. I did photograph the area over the small creek that spills over the hillside (it runs underneath the Duke of Gloucester Street through a pipe) next to the coffee house, and I found that it too had some activity in and around the foliage that flanked each side of the creek. Keep in mind that apparitions hardly ever appear as clearly or as completely as they do in the window glass in the homes and buildings—the glass must be some kind of conduit that enables them to make an appearance without as much of the misty distortion that I typically see in the apparitions that appear in the street. The number of faces in and around the creek may give credence to the running water theory; notice that the first photo shows the vegetation on the left side of the creek, and you can readily see the streaking white light of moving ghosts, with the partial faces that I found within these streaking apparitions when I zoomed in on these areas of the photo.

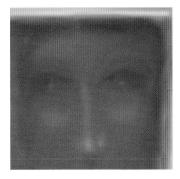
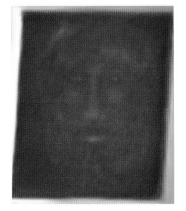
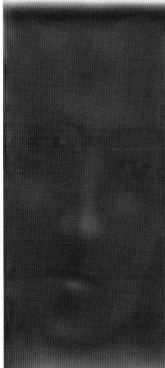
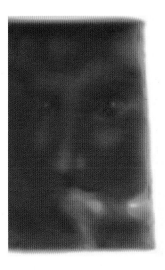

Here are the four clearest faces of the many ghosts that seem to haunt this newly rebuilt landmark in Colonial Williamsburg.

The Anthony Hay Cabinet Shop

The second building in this chapter, the Anthony Hay Cabinet Shop, has flowing water running under its west wing and may reinforce the idea that running water amplifies paranormal activity. The original building was built sometime between 1745 and 1756; this part of the shop was next to the creek and has a closed foundation. An extension to the west was built during the 1760s right over top of the creek on top of brick piers. In addition to the cabinets and furniture that were built here, a good portion of Hay's business came from making coffins (you can see one on display when you enter the shop). I do not know if that fact relates in any way to the paranormal presence in this building, or if it's mostly just due to the running water or the history of the

This is one of many of the photos that I took of the small creek that runs next to the Charlton Coffee House. Notice the streaking white apparitions that have blurred some of the foliage around the creek (you can't actually see the creek because it's surrounded by the tall wildflowers and weeds).

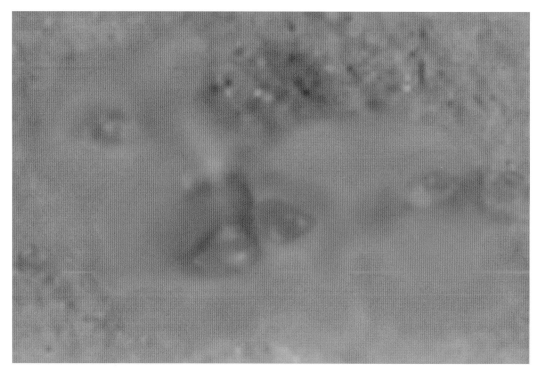

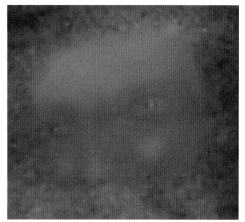

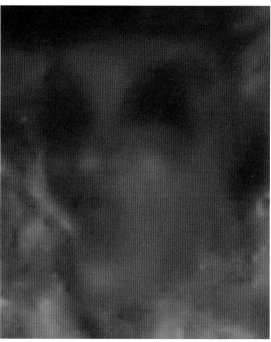

In the photo of the creek that runs alongside the Charlton Coffee House (on the previous page), here are some of the partial faces that I found within the visible white streaks.

Here is a shot of the Anthony Hay Cabinet Shop;
notice that the west wing on the left is built on top of
pillars so that the creek can flow underneath.

grounds. A residence (built in the early eighteenth century) with a separate kitchen (1780s?) was also on this site and existed until sometime between 1810 and the 1820s. Anthony Hay had the cabinet shop from 1756 to 1770, when he died, and Edmund Dickinson ran the shop from 1771 until 1778, when he died. Then the shop was used as a public armory in 1779, until it was taken down before 1782. So this shop only had two owners, plus several workers who would have worked with each, so I would not expect to capture a lot of paranormal activity with my camera—besides the fact that this building is on a backstreet in Williamsburg and does not receive near the traffic that the Duke of Gloucester Street does. So my question is, would this building attract the ghosts from the surrounding area because of the flowing creek, or would I see fewer than normal apparitions because this cabinet shop did not have a lot of workers and was only in existence from 1756 to about 1782 (just twenty-six years)? Would I capture Native Americans who perhaps lived on this land before the eighteenth century, or does this running water theory really have no merit?

The fact that the cabinet shop is poorly lit at night lowered my expectations even more—as I've discussed before I believe artificial light as well as moonlight gives apparitions the energy to appear with greater clarity. I was surprised to see as many faces as I did in the cabinet shop—more than I expected. A lot of them were not very clear, and I left them out, but here are the ones that made an appearance clear enough for this book. As for the running water connection to paranormal activity, I'm going to need more evidence, but from the photographic results of these two buildings I think that it seems plausible . . .

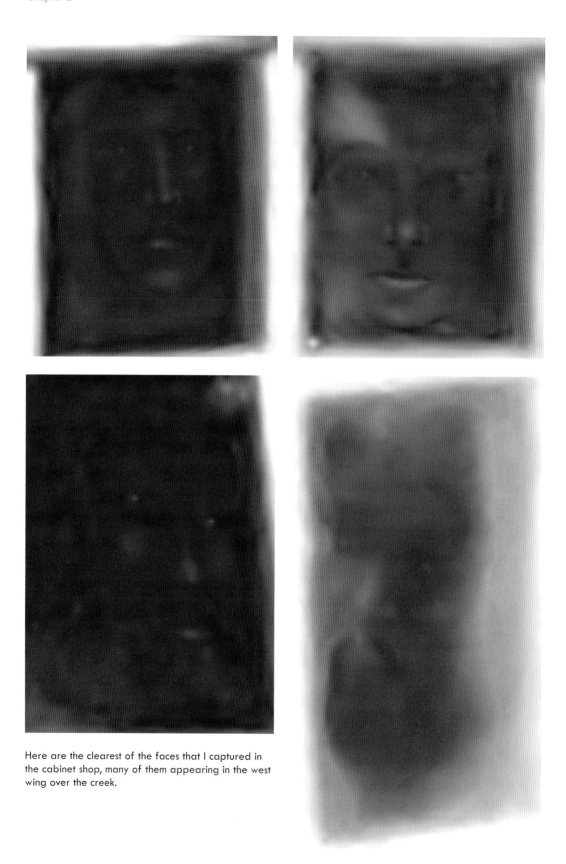

Here are the clearest of the faces that I captured in the cabinet shop, many of them appearing in the west wing over the creek.

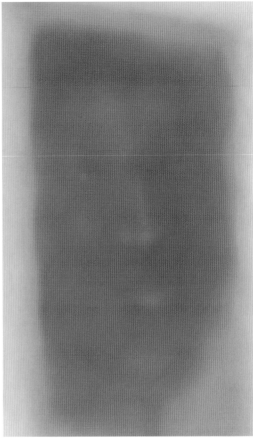

THE EVERHARD HOUSE

What If Your Decision Was Love . . . or Marriage?

History

This is an original home built in 1718, by the first "keeper" of the powder magazine, John Brush. Colonial Williamsburg will usually name a home after the person in possession of the house during the 1770s up through the Revolutionary War, which is why this home is known as the Thomas Everard House. Not only that, but Everard was an example of what America came to symbolize: a land of opportunity where hard work and perseverance will be rewarded. Thomas became an orphan at the age of ten, and was placed in an orphanage by his uncle. This orphanage, called Christ's Hospital, had the foresight to teach the children not only how to read and write, but more importantly a vocation. Thomas was taught how to "cast accounts," so that when he was released at the age of sixteen, his uncle was able to secure him an apprenticeship in America to Matthew Kemp.

Kemp served as clerk in the Secretary's Office, clerk of the General Court, clerk of James City County, and clerk of the Committee for Propositions and Grievances of the House of Burgesses. Everard was a diligent and hardworking apprentice, and within a year of completing his apprenticeship, he obtained his first public appointment to the position of clerk of the courts of Elizabeth City County. Everard would have other appointed public positions as well as serve in many other public offices, including clerk of the York County court from 1745 until his death in 1781, deputy clerk of the General Court, clerk of the Secretary

of the Colony's office, mayor of Williamsburg (he served two one-year terms), and was a member of the Court of Directors of the Public Hospital. Cathy Hellier, a Colonial Williamsburg Foundation historian, researched Everard's work during his tenure as clerk of the York County Court, and she discovered the work ethic of the orphan boy from London: Whereas most county clerks would pass off work orders to assistant clerks, Everard's signature was on hundreds of these documents, attesting to his commitment to his work.

Everard, through his hard work and diligence, became a wealthy landowner, purchasing 1,136 acres in Brunswick County (in the western part of Virginia) and as many as 600 acres in James City County. His wealth enabled him to marry Diana Robinson, a woman from a prominent family, and afforded him a number of slaves. He had two slaves that wore *livery* (a special uniform worn by a servant) just to answer the door, and two others to accompany him on his carriage ride to the York County Court.

The Ghost of a "Fateful Day"?

After quite a few attempts at photographing the Everard House and coming up with just a few hexagon-shaped orbs, I found a very sad-looking face in one of the outbuildings of the house—perhaps one of the slaves that worked at the house? I noticed the eyes immediately when I zoomed in on the windows, and it made me wonder why this soul was looking out the window with such a profoundly forlorn look; what happened?

A later attempt would yield lots of faces—some fully formed and some that could use a little more detail. I have heard that the home is haunted, but I can never get specific firsthand experiences. Some of the faces look female to me, and because of that I wonder if one of them belongs to the woman who etched something into the windowpane of a downstairs window: "Oh fateful day!" Since it would require a diamond to etch this phrase into the glass, most people surmise that the person responsible is female—perhaps on her wedding day. People have been trying to second-guess the meaning of that inscription for many years, and an unhappy young woman being pushed into marrying a man that she did not love seems to be the most logical and the most frequent assumption. Many of the ghost tours tell this story as part of the legacy of the President's House at the College of William and Mary, but according to a Williamsburg employee, the fateful message was inscribed on a windowpane at the Everard House.

Although the glass has since been moved into the safety of a museum or warehouse, perhaps the writer has been left behind forever at the home where she left the foreboding inscription about her future.

Many ask if arranged marriages existed in the eighteenth century, and for the most part, the answer is "No!" Parents did, however, expect to be consulted about a possible marriage partner, and the children were expected to select someone from their social class. Parents did have the ability to deny marriage to a child under the age of twenty-one, usually daughters, because young men typically did not marry until they were in their mid-twenties and had an established job. A young woman would marry anywhere

Here is the Everard House, for the longest time a house that I knew was haunted but could get no photographic proof. But then one evening . . .

from as young as fifteen to her early twenties, but generally the age was the late teens. (In 1763, English law set the minimum age of marriage at sixteen; before this law was enacted, the church would allow girls as young as twelve to be married and boys as young as fourteen.) Another way a parent could control who their child/children married was to cut off the purse strings or even threaten to write them out of their will. This worked for Daniel Custis, who was in his early forties before his father consented to let him marry Martha Dandridge (who would later become Martha Dandridge Custis Washington). If a young woman had an opportunity as young as fifteen to marry a great prospect, especially if she would be marrying up a social class,

you might find her parents pushing her into a union that she did not want. Keep in mind that even when it was the Capital of Virginia, Williamsburg was a relatively small town, and people of a marrying age had a limited amount of prospects.

So here we are at the home of Thomas Everard, a former orphan who worked very hard to attain wealth and prominence in Williamsburg (and who married up, I might add). Could it be someone in his family who was forced to marry against his or her will? Or am I taking you in a completely different direction from the intent of the message, "Oh fateful day"? Perhaps you can decide for yourself after gazing at some of the faces that haunt this original eighteenth-century house.

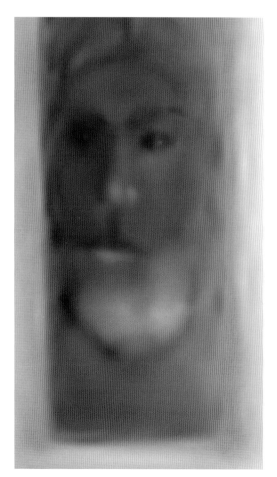

These two faces, the first that I found at the Everard House, appear from the beards to have been from the nineteenth century around the Civil War period when beards were popular.

Here are some of the more normal faces from the Everard House—possibly eighteenth century because of the lack of facial hair, although they could be from the twentieth century as well.

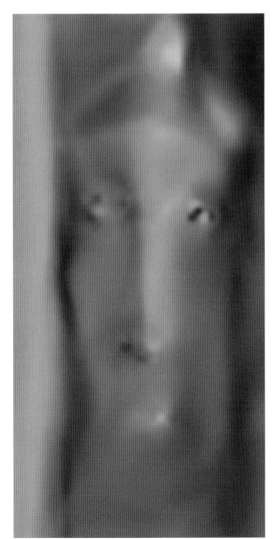

This bizarre, gold-colored face still has me scratching my head, and is that some sort of hat on his or her head?

WHAT ABOUT MY HOUSE?

Living with Multiple Ghosts . . .

You knew it would have to come up—it was inevitable; once I learned how to photograph ghosts and found their ubiquitous presence, I would have to answer this question: Am *I* living with ghosts? I had to first ask myself if I could live with the answer once I knew; and if I know—would *they* know that I know? Would that open the doors to some unwanted, if not frightening paranormal activity? Those in my family who knew of my project were curious, too—and then there were those who did not want to know. Yes, I had trolled the streets of several different places in the wee hours of the night hunting ghosts; I even went into the pitch-black woods hunting for Civil War ghosts around long-forgotten, abandoned battlefields and redoubts—oftentimes alone. But this was something different—it was my personal space; it was where I slept. After several months of going back and forth, weighing the pros and cons of this decision, I took my camera out and photographed my abode.

The History

Before I go on, here's a little background on the road where I live: Four different armies marched on this road (five if you consider that the American "Continentals" were really a separate army from the French—even though they were on the same side), and you never know how many of the wounded fell and were buried along the way. Cornwallis marched the British troops on this road, and General LaFayette closely shadowed him. The signs along the road call it the Washington/Rochambeau route, with both the British and then later the combined American/French forces ending up at Yorktown for the final battle of the Revolutionary War. In 1862, after the May 5th Battle of Fort Magruder (or the Battle of Williamsburg—whichever you prefer to call it), the Confederate forces in Williamsburg quietly withdrew from their redoubts during the night, moving along this road northwest towards Richmond. The Union army would soon follow, establishing a headquarters just up the road from my house at one of the finest plantation homes in all of Virginia—a place frequented by George Washington—Eltham Plantation, home of the Bassett family. My reluctant psychic does not like to drive down this road, because in a certain tree-covered section she sees bloody men in dark-blue uniforms walking arm-in-arm down the road, weary, some next to death, as if they are locked into an endless march through time towards Richmond. Just down the road a couple of miles is a place called Makemie Woods, where the ghost of a Civil War nurse is said to still roam at night. With all of this history, the house has the potential to be occupied by phantoms of the past, but is it?

The Ghosts

May I respond with a resounding yes; my house has ghosts all around it! I found two dominant spherical torches overhead, and around the outside perimeter of my house I found more apparitions, the exception being on the left side of the house where I have counted (depending on the photo) anywhere from five to ten apparitions. Among them I discovered an enormous apparition on my back deck right next to the dining room, and a beautiful geo-light formation on every side of the house. After I took the photos and processed them, I slept a little uneasy through the first night. A couple days later, I went into the bathroom at night and wondered if the cold chill that I got came from the air conditioner vent in the floor, was it my imagination running wild, or was it one of the phantoms that I photographed? Some in my family even suggested that I brought them home from Williamsburg with me! How could that happen?

It has now been several months since I've taken the photos, and nothing seems to have changed. They are still there, but rather innocuous—with the one exception being that someone saw a dark figure walk from the bathroom into a walk-in closet and disappear. I guess that we can peacefully coexist with the ghosts, although I try not to think too much about it. I have heard things go bump in the night, as well as doors opening and closing in the upstairs (when I was downstairs), but I have not seen any dark figures—and I'm kind of glad. Another person in my family has witnessed a young woman with long brown hair, a white top with a long brown dress who seems very anachronistic—dating back perhaps about 200 years or more—in the dining room (right next to the gigantic apparition on the deck). Upon realizing that someone actually saw her, she made eye contact and then quickly turned and disappeared through a closed door—yes, she walked right through it! I haven't seen the young woman myself, but I'm happy that she is not a frightening entity, just a rather normal-looking woman out of a

centuries-old time capsule. Since that first appearance, she has appeared one other time, this time extending her arm out to a sleepy young boy to prevent him from tripping over his pet. He had gotten up in the middle of the night to get his mother a glass of water, and his Great Pyrenees dog had followed him out of the bedroom and laid across his return path, waiting as the boy got a glass of water out of the kitchen. On his return with a full glass of water, the boy would have fallen over the oversized pet and possibly injured himself had not the helpful ghost extended her arm to warn him. His sleepy, half-closed eyes grew wide with surprise and a little fear as he realized that the arm blocking his path belonged to the ghost of what appeared to be a colonial woman. Once again, upon being seen, the ghost completely disappeared in a millisecond.

I will attribute a third story about a paranormal event to this ghost not because she appeared—she did not. But it happened in the kitchen—part of the area that she haunts. A mother and her two teenage daughters came to live with us for a "week," but it ended up being three months, and it was a strain on the budget to support three extra people. In the third month, one of the daughters got up in the middle of the night and went downstairs to the kitchen to get a drink of milk. She took a glass out of the kitchen cabinet, opened the refrigerator, and got out the gallon of milk to fill her glass. After filling her glass on the counter, she turned around and opened the refrigerator to place the gallon back in. While she was putting the gallon of milk back in, the glass of milk that she just poured levitated up above her head, and the entire contents of the glass was emptied on top of the girl's head. The frightened teen ran back upstairs, still dripping with milk, to tell her mother about the supernatural event, all the while insisting that they had to get out of this haunted house. They were gone within a week;

and it makes me wonder how observant ghosts are. Did our ghost know about the strain on our budget? Did she know that pouring the milk over the girl's head would be enough to motivate the mother to get a place of her own?

A second apparition that has been seen is a man in a modern suit that is standing in the hallway next to the stairs. Now this one is a bit of a mystery because this house is about fifteen years old and no one has died here. The house is built on wooded property that had not been built on before—as far as we know. We are the third family to live in it, and with no evidence of any recent deaths on the property, it's an enigma to speculate where the man in the suit came from. The most logical explanation I can think of is that he was killed in an automobile accident along the road, and was attracted to the light at the house.

A Three-Year-Old's Invisible Friend

I do have another intriguing story of a young man in my family who would like to remain anonymous. When this young man was about three years old, he had an imaginary playmate, and he could be heard carrying on a conversation in his bedroom with this person. Whenever his mother would inquire to whom he was speaking, he would always say what we thought was, "I'm talking to the *man*." Now this response had frightened his mother, especially after learning that construction on a mall just a few hundred feet from their house was halted because an ancient Indian burial ground had been unearthed. His mother had no idea who this "man" could be, and it frightened her not knowing who he was or what he wanted with her son. Well the conversations with the invisible playmate continued, and one afternoon the boy's grandmother came into the room.

Her grandson immediately responded, "Awwww, you scared away the man."

She replied, "What man?"

The boy answered, "The man knows you!"

Now the grandmother was freaked out, and the mother and the grandmother both began to panic from the implications of an unseen entity talking to their grandson/son. They began discussing what they could do, and moving away was debated. Although what the boy said in these conversations was innocuous, they had no idea what the invisible entity was saying to the boy, and that unknown factor frightened them. Finally, an answer came when the mother brought the boy to our house, and she was standing in the hallway holding him. On the wall in the hallway are a number of pictures of our family, and the boy looked at one and exclaimed:

"There's my ma'am!"

"Where's your man?' His mother responded incredulously.

"No, not man. *Ma'am!*" he corrected her. "She's right there!"

The boy pointed to a photograph of his great-grandmother, whom he had never seen or met. "That's my ma'am." (The boy had been taught to address people that he did not know as sir and ma'am.)

"That's who you talk to in your room all the time?"

"Yeah; she plays with me. She said she knows you. She said she loves you, you know!" he said matter-of-factly.

His grandmother asked him if he saw her in any other photos on the wall, and he correctly pointed her out in three other photographs. It has been a few years since this happened, and the boy has no recollection of what we thought was his imaginary playmate. It makes me wonder—did I have an imaginary playmate that has slipped away from my memory? Was that person a relative from my past? Has this happened to anyone else in my family? Why do we forget something as profound as that? Do our imaginary friends make us forget? Have you ever asked your family if you had an imaginary friend?

As more and more people discover what I have been doing with my time and the publication of my books, they ask me if my house is haunted. When they learn that it is and the prevalence of ghosts, the next statement is fishing for a possible response from me: "Maybe I should have you come out and check if there are any ghosts at my house . . ." Yes, I've gone to several of my friends homes, and yes I have discovered ghosts at some of them! Now that you know the plethora of paranormal presences in and around Williamsburg, I hand off the same inquiry to you: Are there any ghosts attached to your house?

A Gathering of Ghosts . . . Over Me

Finally, I would like to tell you about an experience that I had recently, and I have no recollection of it. I was lying sound asleep in my bed when whispering woke my wife—but she could not make out what was being said. She looked over to see a large group of ghosts, somewhere between twenty and thirty, gathered around me as I slept. Even though she was now wide awake and looking at this otherworldly scene, she could hear them whispering amongst themselves and still could not make out what they were saying. There were ghosts of all shapes and sizes, male and female, some recognizable human forms and other wispy forms of white light, most of them standing, but some of them floating over top of me. She was so frightened by what she saw she wanted to scream, but was even more frightened at how they might respond. She turned away from me as quietly as she could, sliding the blanket over her head so that she no longer saw the ghostly gathering. Unable to sleep, she lay frozen in fright and fear for what seemed like hours. She finally mustered the courage to turn back over to see if they still surrounded me, and as she did she made a noise as if she was awakening. As she turned over, it was as if she frightened the ghosts—and they all moved with lightning speed up through the bedroom ceiling as if there was some invisible portal to another dimension. The next day she confronted me about the paranormal assembly that surrounded my sleeping self, first asking if I realized what was happening.

"No, I have no recollection of the meeting. As far as my conscious mind, I don't believe I even dreamed about such a gathering. There may be something buried deep in my subconscious that I cannot access . . ."

Then all her fears came out. "You are messing with something you don't understand. You may be drawing them here—I think that they think you can help them. You need to lay off the ghost hunting for a while! You might be putting us in danger!"

I responded by saying that it is quite evident from my photographs that there are a lot of ghosts around this house and grounds. I think they have been here for quite some time. They could go as far back as the Indian massacres of 1622 (I mentioned this because of the woman that shows up in the doorway between the kitchen and the laundry room that I have already mentioned, as well as an old woman who was seen looking in the window from the back deck just recently.) There could also have been deaths and burials on this property from any one of the four different armies that marched this road. Perhaps they do think that I can help them; but I have never indicated that idea—I just take their photographs. But I did not bring them here; they've occupied this land long before we even thought of moving here.

Because we are dealing with the unknown, I can't say that anything that I said helped to ease my wife's apprehension. What I do know is that although they are here, they are not malevolent, and they do not try to frighten us. When they are seen, they seem to be shocked that they have been recognized, and they quickly disappear. It's almost as if they are as frightened of us as we are of them, which is odd because at one time they were one of us. I have to admit, if we had the types of apparitions as those at the Peyton Randolph House, I would be concerned for my family's safety and sanity. But here I think we are dealing with lost souls who might want to be discovered by the living, as well as seeking a way out of their existence in what I perceive to be a limbo—but then again, what do I know?

One thing that comes to my mind after seeing these geometric shapes of what some scientists call an *electromagnetic consciousness* is the most recent hypothesis on this phenomenon put forth by Dr. Susan Pockett in 2012: One necessary characteristic of a conscious field of electromagnetic radiation is a three-dimensional spatial structure: The essence of the proposal is that in the radial direction (perpendicular to the surface of the cortex) conscious fields will have a surface layer of negative charge above two deeper layers of positive charge, separated by a distinct neutral layer. The next few pages are teeming with three-dimensional shapes—conscious electromagnetic fields?

Visible and Invisible Light

I have been asked if I use a full-spectrum camera (a camera that records both visible and invisible light); as any good investigator would, I make use of all available technology, including a full-spectrum camera. Each place, each ghost, and each photograph is different. What I do sometimes to get the best possible photo is to blend photos taken from different cameras of the same subject. But as you can see on the next few pages, apparitions seem to, for the most part, give off more light from the invisible side of the spectrum than from its visible counterpart. In other words, when you look at the apparitions taken with the full-spectrum camera, you will notice that they are dominated by the colors red and violet. The extreme ends of the light spectrum, made up of infrared and ultraviolet light, are invisible to the human eye but are invaluable to a paranormal investigator. I have such an example on the coming pages; using a visible-spectrum camera I found nothing in my living room—but I found a glowing light on the drapes and apparitions in the window with the full-spectrum camera. (This is the same place where a large, opaque apparition hangs outside on the back deck and where someone in my family spotted the face of an old woman looking into the living room.) Conversely, the photographs taken with a camera registering only light from the visible-spectrum, is considered by many to be more beautiful. Take a look at just some of the apparitions around and above my house on the following pages; which do you prefer? Visible spectrum or full spectrum? Then take a look at the faces, which can be captured with both types of cameras: The first two faces, showing up very pink, were taken with the full-spectrum camera; the other faces were taken with a visible-spectrum camera.

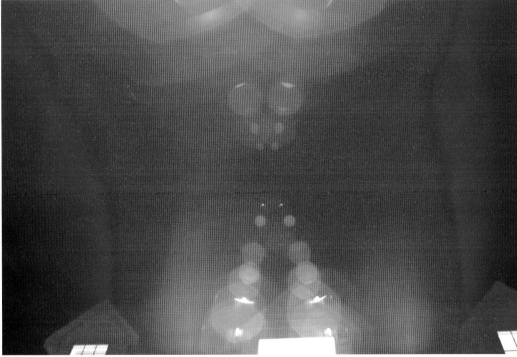

Compare the results of a visible-spectrum photograph verses the full-spectrum counterpart of the same apparitions that occupy the space over my house. Do you notice how much more ultraviolet and infrared light these apparitions emit than the wavelengths from the visible light spectrum?

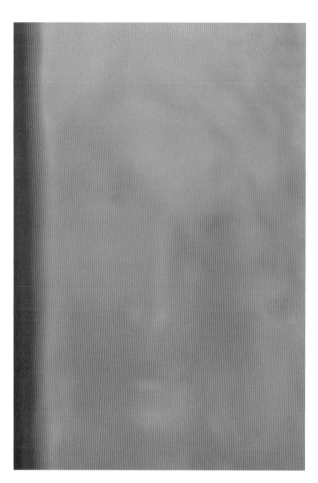

This is the clearest of the two photos at the back of the house; the long hair and the clean-shaven face suggests the eighteenth century.

This was in a nearby windowpane from the first photo—just not as much facial detail.

The photo was taken from the inside of the house, and this feminine face showed up in the glass on the back door. I think it's a different woman from the one in colonial costume that stands at the dining room door.

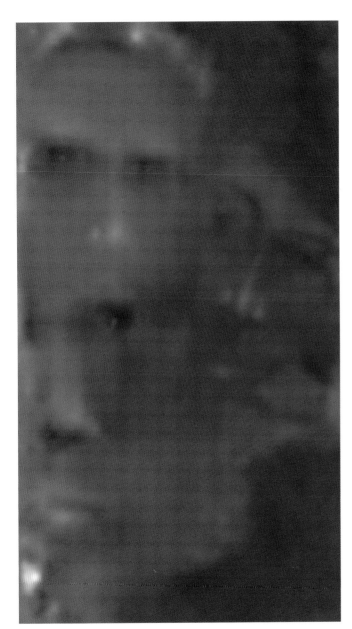

Finally, these two faces showed up in the same window at the very bottom just peeking above the windowsill.

This was captured on the outside of the dining room window, and the two sets of eyes on the left look very similar— I'm thinking that either the same face appeared and then reappeared (they can move incredibly fast!), or that it's two brothers.

THE PEYTON RANDOLPH HOUSE

Meet the New Faces . . . From the Dark Side

The Peyton Randolph House continues to surprise, and I have returned with new photos and stories from this house because it generates so much interest—with its long-held title of "Williamsburg's most haunted." Since I have given the historical background in the first book, I won't repeat that for this chapter on the home named after the man first given the moniker *father of our country*—long before Washington. New faces and pairs of eyes continue to appear in the windows—from the back of the house. Take a look at the new faces—some of them looking quite malevolent—and new stories from the dark side of Williamsburg.

A former interpreter who worked there in the 1980s told another supernatural story about the Peyton Randolph House. Since he no longer works there, he is not afraid to tell of his firsthand experience with one of the more menacing ghosts in this house. (If you recall from the first book, at the time, it was grounds for dismissal/firing if any Colonial Williamsburg employee discussed the paranormal and/or admitted to having a para-experience in the homes or buildings they worked in.) It was the end of the day, and he and the female interpreter he was working with were getting ready to leave. While he was doing some paperwork at the desk, she was going through the procedure of closing all of the shutters to the windows on the east side of the house. The direct sunlight coming into the rooms can damage some of the artifacts, like paintings and furniture, particularly anything that was made with cloth, so

this was a regular closing requirement of all employees at the Randolph House. He could hear her as she closed the shutters in the first window, but as she left the room, he could hear another set of footsteps in addition to hers. The footsteps were much heavier than hers, and he had not been informed about any presence there—human or paranormal. So he thought that there was someone else in the house—perhaps a tourist who came in late and who had not seen that the flag had been taken down. (A flag outside a building in Colonial Williamsburg means that the building is open that particular day for tourists. Different buildings/houses are open on different days, so you have to consult the guide you are given when purchasing tickets to see what is open on that day.) So as the interpreter got up from his desk to go investigate the extra set of footsteps, he heard a blood-curdling scream coming from the female interpreter, and he rushed to the room that she was in, thinking that she was being attacked. When he got to the room she was in, she was the only person in the room, but she was shaking and sobbing. When she settled down enough to tell her story, she explained what had happened.

She had just finished closing the shutters to the windows in the room she was in, when she heard a series of heavy footsteps stomping their way to her. As she turned around from the window she could see what looked like an angry, scowling man coming right for her. The man was dressed in eighteenth-century clothing, and she let out a scream because she thought he was going to attack her. But just as he got to her, he disappeared into thin air, leaving her shaking and rattled, and as she told the story, she kept looking around her to make sure that the enraged paranormal occupant of the house did not return. The male interpreter asked her if she was okay, or if she would like to talk to someone about her experience. She immediately began to shake her head no even before he was done with his sentence, and said immediately after he finished, "I can't tell anyone—they will fire me! You can't tell anyone either, not unless you don't need this job! Please, let's just hurry up and finish locking up and get out of here as fast as humanly possible! But don't leave me—I don't want to be alone if that ghost comes back after me." So they finished up closing the shutters together and nervously left the building, the frightened woman looking all around as she walked out of that house, ready to make a run for the door should the confrontational phantom return.

A final story about this house demonstrates that not all of the phantoms here are malevolent—just a little mischievous. The fire alarm went off in the area to the far right (at one time a separate house, until Randolph built the two-story section that connected to it), and access to this separate living area was blocked off from the main house. It was an empty cottage (directly connected to the rest of the house, but with separate entrances and no inside access to the main house from this part) where two sisters formerly lived, and both security and the fire department now discovered that there was no key to that part of the Randolph House—and of course, they needed immediate access to determine where the fire was. They searched in several different places for the key and found that no one seemed to have one for this part of the house. The security officer discovered that if he manipulated the window he could loosen the locking pegs and open it. The security team and the firefighters in full turnout gear crawled through the window to quickly search for the fire in this priceless eighteenth-century house. In the middle of the floor was a fire extinguisher that was spent. They had to recheck the whole perimeter: No sign of forced entry—everything was locked.

Here is the rub—a physical impossibility as far as we know: The residue from the fire extinguisher never broke the threshold of any of the doorways (there was a perfect line of residue across each threshold, as if this unseen force was somehow able to place invisible tape across it and keep it completely out of

The front of the Peyton Randolph House on a bright spring day—but one window shows the ominous side of the house—even in the light.

the next room!); just the one room contained the contents of the fire extinguisher. The pin was never found, but the fire extinguisher was sitting in the middle of the floor, which was bare of any residue underneath.

About a year later, the security officer, Chuck Rayle, spoke with the acting chief that was on call that night as they worked with a heat-seeking thermal unit (something that is used by firefighters and ghost hunters) at the stables of Colonial Williamsburg. The chief in charge that evening admitted with a great deal of reluctance: "It was not of this world; it was not human. God, I hate saying 'paranormal,' but that's the only explanation." There was no smoke and no fire, so did the fire extinguisher set off the alarm? Was this a poltergeist prank, or did the ghost actually prevent a fire from starting?

There are new and somewhat sinister apparitions in the windowpanes in the downstairs back part of this large house. The first face was very dark, and it looked very stern—if not angry— with glowing eyes. If you recall the apparitions at the jailhouse (the classic Halloween representation of ghosts, with a glowing white face and black features for the eyes and sometimes a mouth, with the nose optional), you will find something very similar in the two subsequent photographs. The third apparition had a strange appearance, with large, "bug" eyes, and again, a very dark appearance. I also captured a second set of eyes on the side of the house—another malevolent entity, or just the same one with a slightly different but equally intimidating stare? Two "firsts" happened to me this time around at Williamsburg's most haunted: One is that I captured the same face twice on two different nights; the second is that I captured a window full of classic whites in the broad daylight—and I wasn't even trying to capture anything paranormal— I was just hoping for a great shot of the house on a mostly sunny, warm spring day. It's almost as if they know . . .

This crop and close-up of one of the windows from this eighteenth-century house compels you to realize why some say it's one of the most haunted houses on the East Coast. It makes you wonder just how many souls are locked in this house . . .

Whenever I get a little complacent, or when I seem to be getting the same old same old faces in other parts of the city, I can always count on the Peyton Randolph House to get the really bizarre visages—or to find a set of eyes to send a chill down your spine. I think they are trying to let me know that they are watching me . . .

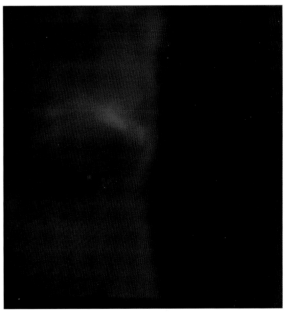

This forlorn face was captured on the side of the Peyton Randolph House on the night of an October full moon.

The Peyton Randolph House continues to show new faces that are ominous and threatening.

On the side of the Peyton Randolph House, for the first time, I have captured what appears to be the same face twice: Compare the face in the top left windowpane to the darker face in the next photo. What do you think—is it the same ghost?

THE HAUNTED ELEMENTARY SCHOOL

Mathew Whaley and His Pauper Friend or
the Two Murdered Boys?

Would you send your young child to an elementary school that is rumored to be haunted? Parents in Williamsburg, Virginia, have been sending their children to the Mathew Whaley Elementary School for quite some time—most of them acutely aware of the paranormal activity. Some of them do not believe the rumors, and some believe the rumors but also contend that all paranormal activity is innocuous. To understand the paranormal activity in this school, you have to go back in time.

History

Mathew Whaley was born to a wealthy couple in the late seventeenth century; the only son of James and Mary Page Whaley was born in Williamsburg in 1696, just three years before it became the capital of the Virginia colony. He was educated at his mother's small grammar school, held in the family's backyard. Mathew was the product of a very wealthy family, and at that time, social classes did not fraternize with each other. However, the boy's mother may have looked the other way when he became friends with a very poor boy—some say a slave boy. It is rumored that she even began to teach the boy to read and write—in secret.

Both boys were stricken by a virus or disease at the same time with the same result: Young Mattey died at the age of nine years (1705), and his tomb can be seen in the graveyard right outside the Bruton Parish Church in Williamsburg. It is rumored that Mattey's friend was buried nearby in an unmarked grave, paid for by his kindhearted mother. Mathew's father, who helped Governor Francis Nicholson design the city of Williamsburg, is said to have died just three years later, in 1708. Mrs. Whaley returned to England, but before doing so left an endowment for a free school to educate the poor and named in Mathew's honor, appointing Bruton Parish Church to manage the school and the endowment.

The first manifestation of the Mathew Whaley School had a schoolhouse, a stable, and a headmaster's house, but this disappeared sometime during the Revolutionary War. After the Civil War, the English court wrote to the wardens of the Bruton Parish Church regarding the trust fund set up by Mrs. Whaley, who referred the matter to the College of William and Mary—because the college was operating a grammar school for the impoverished children of Bruton Parish. The college held classes at the Brafferton Building (remember this building from the first book?) until a building was erected, in 1870, on the grounds of the former Governor's Palace—even using the bricks from the burned mansion. Eventually, the building was turned over to the city of Williamsburg, and a new public school building was constructed on the site. There was a great deal of angst in Williamsburg when the Colonial Williamsburg Foundation wanted to buy the property to tear down this new school building and restore the Governor's Palace. Rockerfeller had to promise the very finest school building money could buy before the people of Williamsburg would consent to selling their recently built school building and razing it to the ground. Finally, with the city's consent, the property was sold to Colonial Williamsburg, and a third building was begun in 1929, and completed the next year on a nearby property to the Governor's Palace; this school would again bear the name of Mathew Whaley. This building, occupied by both the living and the dead, still stands today.

A Controversy: Who Really Haunts This School?

Williamsburg James City County presently uses the building as an elementary school, so it's quite obvious who the living occupants of the school are—but who are the dead ones? That question has been up for debate for some time—with two completely different answers. Some, of course, say that the school is haunted by young Mathew Whaley and his pauper (or slave) friend, while others point to a more recent tragedy in the school's history: the death of two young African American boys in the early 1960s at the hands of an anti-desegregationist—someone who would kill children to prevent or stall the government's mandate that blacks and whites must attend the same schools. Most people in Williamsburg prefer the Mathew Whaley story rather than the lesser-known story of the two African American boys who were murdered—in fact, most people in Williamsburg are completely unaware of this dark chapter in the city's history. There is even a bronze sculpture of the young Mathew Whaley on a bench in front of the school, but no mention of the two murdered boys.

Unless the present elementary school sits on the grounds of the original Whaley house (which is not known at this point), I am inclined to believe that the school is haunted by the two African American boys who were murdered by one or more pro-segregationists. These two boys actually had a connection to the school, whereas young Mathew Whaley and his poor, or perhaps slave, friend had none. From my understanding of hauntings, a spirit must have had a physical connection to a house, the ground, or an object in order to haunt it. What do you think?

I thought this (and wrote it) even before I had a photo of the faces in the windowpanes, but at least for me, the photos sealed the deal. Although faces will appear dark (unless they are of the classic white type) no matter what race the individuals were before they passed on, you can usually tell by characteristic facial features what race the person was. Of course that statement can be put to the test with the ambiguity of a mixed-race individual, but note that I said *usually.* Anyway, from the photos I would state that the haunting appears to be the two murdered boys. Notice that the photo of the front of the school demonstrates again how large these apparitions can be, as well as the more compact apparitions taken in the back of the school and on the side. These photos were taken on different days, and so the obvious question I have: Are they two different photos/versions of the same ghost? As for the faces, the first photo makes me think of the two African American boys. I would later discover other faces in other windows, so I will leave it up to you. You've heard the two stories; which story could these faces be connected to?

Mathew Whaley Elementary School front; notice the
faint apparitions, as well as one or more that are
quite large to the far right.

A geo-light apparition that
appeared above the window of
one of the faces on the following
page. My question—are the
geo-light apparitions and the
faces in the windows connected?
Are they part of the same
consciousness?

Even before I took this photo I felt that the haunting was most likely by the two African American boys who were murdered; what do you think after seeing this photo?

This is the clearest face I captured; I'm not sure if this could be one of the two African American boys or not. I've had a suggestion that this might be someone completely different— perhaps Mathew Whaley's friend.

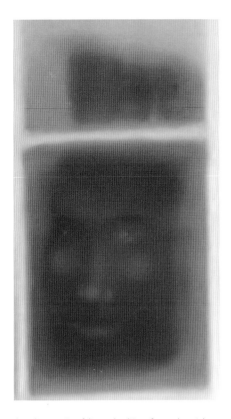

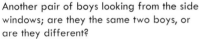

Another pair of boys looking from the side windows; are they the same two boys, or are they different?

Is this a child or an adult? Someone suggested Mathew Whaley, but does he look young enough to be a ten-year-old boy?

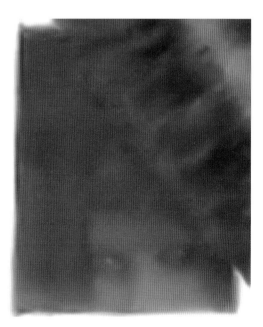

A rather sinister and dark-looking face . . .

Finally, could this be a boy from the twentieth century? The shorter haircut makes me think so . . .

THE GOVERNOR'S PALACE

Royalty, Revolution, and Wraiths

A palatial residence was erected on sixty-three acres of land to house the governor of Virginia, the representative of the British crown, beginning in 1706, and taking sixteen years to complete. Along the way there were a few pauses to the construction as the governor would press the House of Burgesses for more money to complete the project, along with more demands for lavish additions to the already tight budget. The project was finally finished in 1722, under Governor Spotswood: The massive three-story home with a cupola included ornate woodwork, lavish furnishings, a stable, carriage house, kitchen, scullery, laundry, octagonal bathhouse, underground icehouse, and ornamental gardens. The governor's household required a staff of twenty-five slaves and servants to function. The butler played an important role at the palace, determining by any guest's level of importance how close he got to the governor and/or whether the king's representative would even give an audience to the visitor. People who had little to no status would usually not even get in the front door. This residence was first referred to as a "palace" before it was even complete—all the way back in 1714; whether this was out of respect or out of derision (for the runaway costs to the taxpayers) is not known. The Governor's Palace became the gold standard for Virginia's gentlemen farmers to meet or exceed when constructing their plantation homes.

Beginning in 1718 (yes, four years before it was finished), Governor Spotswood took up residence in the palace—along with every royal governor since. But most people will only recognize the names of the final two governors of the independent state of Virginia: Patrick Henry and Thomas Jefferson. The final royal governor, Lord Dunmore, moved out of the palace under cover of darkness and under the guard of the British sailors on June 8, 1775. It was at this point that the magnificent palace's role began to change dramatically until its tragic end: General Charles Lee of the American (Continental) army made the palace his headquarters until it became a military hospital; then it was renovated for Virginia's first American governor, Patrick Henry. Thomas Jefferson succeeded Henry to the office and moved the capital of Virginia to Richmond in 1780. During the Battle of Yorktown, in 1781, the palace became a military hospital for a second time. On December 22, 1781, an arsonist set a fire in the basement that incinerated the palace in just three hours; one of the soldier/patients did not escape the flames. During this stint as a military hospital, 156 soldiers, as well as two women, were buried on the grounds in shallow graves (barely a foot deep) and without caskets. These soldiers remained interred there until archeologist Prentice Duell began to search for the palace foundations in July of 1930. Local curiosity mounted during these excavations, and hundreds of people came to watch—until officials called in guards and then built a fence around the palace grounds while workers unearthed the makeshift cemetery.

The advance buildings for the palace stood until 1862, when Union soldiers knocked them down to utilize the bricks to build chimneys for the officer's huts across town. Two school buildings stood on the palace grounds just in front of its old foundation when Colonial Williamsburg acquired the property from the city in 1928. The palace was meticulously reconstructed using not only artifacts found in the archeological dig, but also Thomas Jefferson's drawings of the floor plans and an engraved plate from England (the Bodleian Library). The reconstructed palace opened in April 1934, and then the reports of hauntings began.

Ghosts Lighting Fires, Invisible Walkers, and a Hanging

A whole family reported seeing the silhouette of a man up in the cupola walking around. A few minutes later a security guard walked out of the palace and they asked him if he was the person they saw; he said that he only walks through the first and second floors. He also said that there wasn't even a floor where they saw the man standing. The observer incorrectly attributed it to a Civil War lookout—as you have already read the palace burned down in 1781; if it was a lookout for any war, it would have had to have been the Revolutionary War.

One surprising ability that ghosts seem to have is to light fires—whether it's a candle or a fireplace—and it makes sense knowing that they are attracted to light. (Knowing this, I can't help but wonder if ghosts have burned down a residence or building that they did not like, especially a building that replaced a previous residence they occupied.) One evening a security guard that I know got a call about a lit candle in the palace on the second floor,

and he and another guard were dispatched to go inside to check out the report—they went in and could find no candle lit. They went back outside, looked up to the second floor as they opened the doors to their vehicle, and saw the candle burning. They went back in, ascended the stairs, and could smell that a candle had just been put out as well as see the residual smoke. They went back outside and looked up to the second floor to see that the candle was lit again. They realized that the ghost(s) was/were playing games with them, and rather than ascending the steps a third time to find the flames extinguished, they left.

Besides the activity within the rebuilt palace, security guards have also reported a lot of paranormal activity on the grounds around the area where the shallow graves were unearthed. Two security officers found someone watching them from behind a tree. When one would go to investigate and shine the flashlight directly on the tree, he would see nothing. But the other officer could still see the ghost from his vantage point and said, "How can you not see him, you're looking right at him?" They traded places and the same thing happened; yet when they both went back to their original vantage point they both could see the figure hiding behind the tree and peeking around. Ironically, the ghost was invisible to them when either of them stood next to it, but when they stood back it was plainly visible!

The same two security officers were at the upper end of the canal on the bridge over the canal. Every once in a while some college students would jump over the wall near the maze and roam the grounds of the Governor's Palace. One officer went to the maze to check that possibility out. About ten minutes later the other officer, waiting at the bridge by the canal, could hear the footsteps of two to three people coming his way. (In the eighteenth century one of the food staples in Williamsburg was oysters, and the crushed shells were used to make garden paths. When a person walks on these paths, a distinct crunching sound is made, more so than when on gravel. The paths around the palace are made of oyster shells.) He assumed that it was college students coming, so he shined his flashlight towards the direction of the footsteps and could see nothing, and the footsteps ceased. He turned it off and footsteps resumed. He nervously waited till the footsteps were just about upon him to again shine his light on the walkers. The footsteps stopped and the flashlight again revealed that nothing visible was creating the noise. Not quite sure what he was dealing with, the security officer warned the para-walkers to be careful. The second officer returned to reiterate an eerily similar story of hearing footsteps, shining the flashlight in the direction of the sounds, and not seeing anyone making the sounds. Perhaps the Revolutionary War soldiers were out for a moonlight march . . .

A final story that is associated with the Governor's Palace is a great one that I have not been able to verify. This too concerns William and Mary students hopping the wall to the grounds of the Governor's Palace, only with a much more morbid ending than the invisible walkers. A pair of young lovers from William and Mary decided to go for a moonlight walk in the gardens of the palace. The male student helped his girlfriend scale the wall, and once she was over the other side, he climbed to the top of the wall. He was just in time to hear the final sound from his girlfriend's mouth—a blood-curdling scream—before a man wielding a scythe dealt her a fatal blow to the neck. The man, a highly unstable mental patient who had escaped the confines of the nearby Eastern State Lunatic Asylum, fled into the darkness of the palace grounds when he realized that he had been seen. Few people tell this haunting story of the hapless victim of a

madman; I can only wonder if she has joined the para-walkers to take that moonlight walk that she missed out on that ominous night.

The ghosts of the Governor's Palace have been quite elusive to my camera, particularly the 156 ghosts of the Revolutionary War veterans who were buried in the mass grave out back. Orbs have appeared in photos in this area, but because there is so much doubt in the public eye that orbs are paranormal in nature, I have left these photos out. I have captured something that I've only seen at the Wren Building overhead—five spherical torches in a line overtop of the cupola, and looking very much like the straight military formation that I discovered at the Wren. It makes me wonder if there is something about the number five, because this is the second time I've encountered this—and you will see a third time in the very next chapter of this book. A most interesting capture was two faces in the same window, but in adjacent windowpanes. One looks as if he is from the twentieth century (because of the short haircut parted on the side), but the nose and mouth area is almost not present. The face actually resembles a representative from the Smithsonian that was present in 1930: Forensic anthropologist Ales Hrdlicka of the Smithsonian Institution visited the Governor's Palace August 19–20, 1930, and examined more than sixty sets of human remains unearthed during the excavation. Upon seeing his photo from the Williamsburg newspaper I was immediately reminded of the apparition on the left windowpane—coincidence? The image on the right pane is a male with a hairstyle from the eighteenth century, and again this face seemed to lack nose and mouth features. Perhaps this is one of the royal governors that presided over the mansion during its heyday. But the most interesting thing is that the ghosts of two men from two different centuries are juxtaposed in the same window—just like the importance of time to the living is juxtaposed against the timelessness of the dead.

One evening I captured four faces in one window, each in a different windowpane. The first one has a continuation of the mystery from my first book: Why do apparitions keep showing up with one light eye and one dark eye? The next face only has one eye visible, so I can't tell if it has the enigmatic characteristic. The third face has this cryptic look, along with an elongated, gaunt visage. The fourth face, for the first time in a window, shows a head, neck, torso, and arms. The head is unnaturally tilted to the side, as is the body, and someone immediately suggested that it looked as if this person was hanged. Since I

have never seen a person that was hung, I don't know for sure, but it certainly appears to be a viable possibility. What do you think; was this man hung?

On yet another evening, when a special program was being held at the Governor's Palace, I captured what appears to be two ghost children standing in front of a Williamsburg interpreter. I captured a face staring at me through the opened gate just a few seconds later. Next are two faces, one appearing over top of another in that competition to be seen. Finally I captured what appears to be a man in a white-powdered wig, and perhaps has the best chance of being the faded portrait of a former governor of Virginia; the question is, which one?

The Governor's Palace has five apparitions in military-like formation over the cupola.

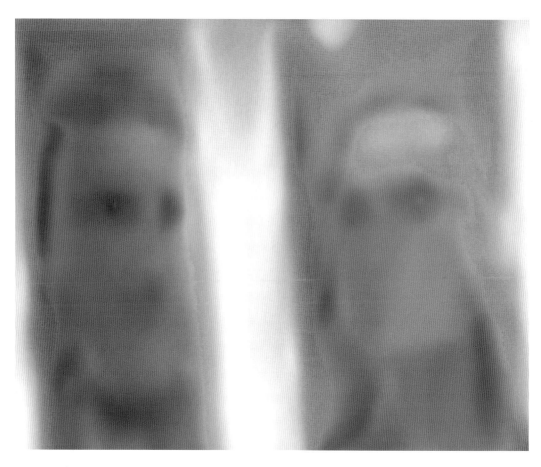

These two faces appeared in adjacent windowpanes; the one on the right appears out of the eighteenth century, and the one on the left is out of the twentieth century.

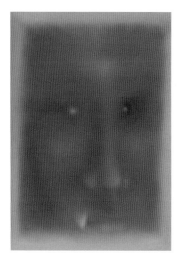

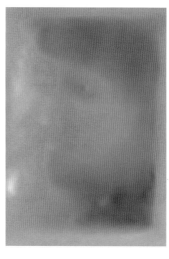

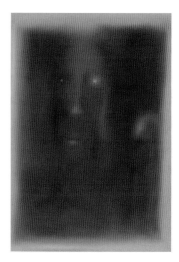

A lone face with one dark eye and one light eye; it never ceases to intimidate!

A face that dominates the window with a pair of eyes appearing at his neck—perhaps a Revolutionary War soldier?

Gaunt seems to be the word that fits both the larger and smaller face; some think Native American.

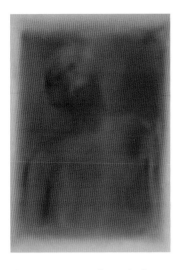

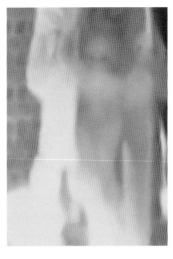

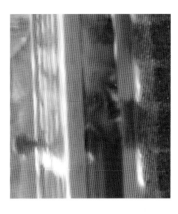

As I took a photo of the people leaving the Governor's Palace, this face appeared in between the main gate and the wall behind the back of a woman in eighteenth-century dress that worked for Colonial Williamsburg.

The most intriguing face of all; notice that the neck is tilted to the side as if he was hanged—what do you think? This is the first head with a torso that appeared in a single windowpane, and the only example of a hanging that I have ever captured!

Two small ghosts, perhaps children, stand in front of one of Colonial Williamsburg's interpreters at the front door of the Governor's Palace.

I can't help but think, because of what appears to be a white-powdered wig, that this may be one of the former royal governors of colonial Virginia. If he is—what a find!

GREEN SPRING ROAD

History

Anthony Wayne, given the moniker "Mad Anthony" for his fiery temperament, was both a Revolutionary War hero and later a man drawn out of retirement by then-President George Washington to fight the Native Americans. I want to relate both Wayne's role in a Revolutionary War battle near Williamsburg and an intriguing ghost story about the general. But first, his role in the Battle of Green Spring: Historical markers across the road from Carlton Farms, a locally owned and operated boarding and riding facility, indicate that the surrounding site is of the Revolutionary War's Battle of Green Spring. According to the Virginia Department of Historical Resources (as seen on the plaques that are mounted at this site), 800 American troops under the command of Brigadier General Anthony Wayne and the Marquis de Lafayette, took on 5,000 British and Hessian troops (hired mercenaries from Germany) on the site of this farm and the surrounding area on July 6, 1781. General Wayne believed that he was only attacking Cornwallis' rear guard, and that the main force was across the James River. He quickly realized that he had made a mistake and that he was outnumbered more than five to one; Wayne did something that may have solidified his nickname "Mad Anthony": He shocked the British forces by charging them, exchanging shots, and then quickly withdrawing his troops under the cover of dusk—which prevented Cornwallis from pursuing and defeating the much smaller American force. This indecisive battle was a

prelude to the siege of Yorktown a few months later, where Cornwallis would concede defeat and end the war. (Let me add that although the Virginia historical markers call the attack a "mistake," the account given at www.ushistory.org indicates that Cornwallis had set up an ambush for the American troops, but Wayne, rather than retreating as expected, shocked the British troops by charging at them. This maneuver caught the British off guard and so confused the ranks that not only did Wayne escape without heavy losses, but he also saved Lafayette's troops from the same trap.)

Green Spring was the home of Governor Sir William Berkeley, and it is not far from this site. Green Spring Road was a road that ran from Jamestown to the Governor's plantation; but it was also a part of a larger thoroughfare that ran from Jamestown Island to the falls on the James River, staying close to the river and linking all of the settlements along the way. The area where this battle took place was originally a large tract of land (3,000 acres) set aside by the Virginia Company to seat tenants who would farm the land and in exchange would give half their profits to cover the expenses of the office of the governor. Virginia governors would also lease this land to other colonists to farm.

Out along this road there is a path for hikers and bicyclists that is paved, and friends of mine told me about getting the sense that they were being both watched and followed. Some even took photos where you could see what looked like hazy apparitions of Native Americans. I did not feel the photos matched the quality of the other photos in this book, so I went out on a quest to get my own. What I discovered across from the battlefield markers, at the well-lit entrances to Carlton Farms, was a group of ghostly apparitions that hovered over the spotlights of the gate. I cannot say who they are—they could be Native Americans, or British, French, or American soldiers from the Battle of Green Spring. One of them could even be "Mad Anthony" Wayne, despite the legendary ghost story about the storied general being in two places in Pennsylvania. One thing I have discovered is that ghosts do not always return to the site of their death; they can also appear at the site of a mistake or regret. Could one of these apparitions be the famous Revolutionary War hero, who was drawn back to the site of a military mistake that he made on this road, perhaps feeling guilty about the men among his ranks who lost their lives here, or is he destined to spend his afterlife pursuing a more morbid activity?

What morbid activity you say? Why, looking for the rest of his body and bones! General Anthony Wayne is probably the only person on this continent who has two official burial places . . . and some of his bones strewn along the 400 miles of road in between. Of course, there is a whole background story to rationally explain the burial plots and the lost bones—and a ghost story to irrationally explain in the aftermath.

This tale begins after the Revolutionary War; in 1792, President George Washington appointed Anthony Wayne as commander-in-chief of the American Army, with a mission to take on and defeat the Indian Confederation that had decimated frontier settlements in the Northwest Territory—essentially the area between Ohio and the Mississippi River. Wayne had to recruit and train a new army; the Revolutionary War had been over for close to a decade and the surviving citizen-soldiers (militias from each state) had returned to their homes and families. By 1796, Wayne had defeated the Indians and signed a peace treaty with them that secured thousands of square miles of land for the young nation. Soon after, he visited Presqu'Isle, a fort on Lake Erie (now the city of Erie, Pennsylvania), where he had a serious gout attack that ended his life. Wayne, only fifty-one, was buried at the foot of the blockhouse's flagpole inside the fort.

Though Wayne was buried in northwestern Pennsylvania, his family lived close to 400 miles away in the eastern part of the state. One of Wayne's daughters (some say Peggy, other versions say Margaretta) persuaded her brother, Isaac, to go and retrieve their father's body, and bring it back home to the family's burial plot at St. David's Church in Radnor, Pennsylvania. It sounds simple enough, right? Isaac would go to Erie, dig up his father's casket, and bring back his father's remains in a carriage to Radnor . . .

But wait! There are two problems: Some say that the locals in Erie were adamant that their beloved general and Revolutionary War hero not be taken away, holding out for two burial plots. But the second problem was that Isaac only had a sulky—the nineteenth-century equivalent to a horse-drawn sub-compact car, with only two wheels and no roof. There was barely enough room for the driver and a passenger; the tiny carriage could only carry a small trunk or box in the back—and definitely incapable of carrying a full-size casket (and Wayne was a big man—about the size of George Washington, who was six-feet-two inches tall). Enter Dr. John Wallace, the very same Pittsburgh physician who was originally called to try to save the ailing general twelve years prior, only to learn that he had died on the very day that he arrived.

General Wayne was disinterred, and Dr. Wallace examined the body; to his dismay the general's body was in an excellent state of preservation, with only one leg showing some decay. To get the body to fit into a container small enough to be transported by Isaac Wayne's sulky, Dr. Wallace would have to do something repugnant to all involved: He would dismember and then boil the flesh off the bones of the body in a large kettle (a known Native American practice), and then pack the bones in a trunk small enough to be carried on the sulky. When his odious task was complete, Dr. Wallace dumped Wayne's flesh, clothing, all of his instruments, and the foul-smelling water back into the coffin and reburied Wayne in his original grave. Isaac left Presqu'Isle with his father's bones packed in a trunk on his sulky for a close-to-400-mile journey over rough, steep trails. (By today's standards, you can hardly call them roads, but today's smoothed and paved version is called Route 322.)[1,2]

According to the legend, the trunk kept falling off of Isaac's sulky due to the terrible road conditions he encountered—some say the young man drove too fast for the road conditions—but the end result was that Isaac lost some of his father's bones along the way. So every New Year's Day, which happened to be General Wayne's birthday, Mad Anthony arises from his grave in Erie at the rebuilt Presqu' Isle Blockhouse (now a museum), whistles for his charger "Nancy," and takes the same route his son Isaac took some 200 years ago to retrieve his lost bones.

So, whether Wayne resides in Erie or is that massive apparition just outside of Williamsburg at the site of his "mistake" at the Battle of Green Spring, I cannot say. But what I can say is that the apparitions hover over the well-lit gate at this site in a military-like order, perhaps in their minds, with or without General Mad Anthony Wayne, they are still fighting the Battle of Green Spring. This is the third time that I have photographed a line of five apparitions in a military-style line, and I wonder if there is any significance to the number five. I have photographed a similar lineup over top the Wren Building at the College of William and Mary and over the Governor's Palace in Colonial Williamsburg; both served as military hospitals during the Revolutionary War. Are there any military experts who can give a logical reason for these phenomena? I would love to know . . .

Now I wonder if these apparitions are British or American troops from the Battle of Green Spring in 1781. Notice the five apparitions above the farm entrance—remember the back of the Wren Building from my first book? The Governor's Palace? There were exactly five apparitions across the top of both buildings, too! Is there something about the number "5" in the paranormal paradigm, or is it just coincidence?

This huge apparition was to the right of the gate; was it perhaps the leader of this group of men who died here? I would have loved to capture a real face at this site . . .

On the other side of the road I heard a rustling in the field, and I photographed the area immediately: It looks like these streaking ghosts were trying to get me to notice them . . .

THE COURTHOUSE OF 1770

Could the Defendants Be on Trial in the Afterlife?

History

The Courthouse of 1770 was started in that year and finished a year later, placed not only in the center of Market Square, but also in the center of town, no doubt a metaphor for observance of the law being a central issue to keeping a city functioning smoothly. Capitol crimes was a term coined from that point on because they were serious crimes that were tried at the Capitol building, whose punishment could be death—capitol punishment, another term coined then. At this courthouse, less serious crimes, what we might call misdemeanors (petty crimes, as well as civil cases), were tried, and many of the corporal punishments were carried out just outside of the courthouse. The whipping post, the stocks (where you had to sit on a very thin, very uncomfortable board with your ankles placed in leg irons), or the pillory (where you placed your head and hands to be locked in a standing position for several hours with your ear lobes nailed to the wood) were all possible punishments for being found guilty in this court. If you were sentenced to either the stocks or the pillory, keep in mind two things: They did not let you out for bathroom breaks, and people could pelt you with eggs, tomatoes, and the like if they so desired—which begs the question, how well are you liked by your neighbors?

In addition to misdemeanor and civil trials, this courthouse was the town center for another important reason: Major announcements were made from the courthouse steps. For example,

Benjamin Waller (a lawyer—remember him from the first book?) read the Declaration of Independence to the citizens of Williamsburg from these very same steps. Another equally important document was read from the courthouse steps on May 1, 1783: The announcement that the Treaty of Paris had been signed, officially ending the Revolutionary War and marking the emergence of a new nation—two years after the British had surrendered at Yorktown.

This courthouse's 160 years of service to the city of Williamsburg and James City County were briefly interrupted by the Civil War's Battle of Williamsburg. First it was a Confederate barracks, then it was converted to a Confederate hospital. When the retreating Rebel army determined that Williamsburg was untenable, they headed for Richmond—taking with them the windows and doors to the courthouse—some conjecture is that perhaps they needed firewood (I know—the windows?). Dr. Alfred Hitchcock (no, not the famous film director, but a Union surgeon during the Civil War) wrote to another surgeon that when he and a team of thirty special surgeons arrived in Williamsburg after the battle (on May 5, 1862) they had to care for about 1,000 Rebel and 500 Union wounded. Makeshift hospitals were made out of the Courthouse of 1770, the Wren Building at the College of William and Mary, four different churches, and many private residences. Who knows how many of the wounded that passed away at the Courthouse still reside there?

Fire gutted the building in 1911, but left the walls standing to be rebuilt with something many in Williamsburg felt was long overdue: Columns were placed under the portico. Some historians believe that a lack of funding kept the courthouse's eighteenth-century builder (called an "undertaker") from adding columns, so they added them when the courthouse was rebuilt (like several other "original" buildings in Williamsburg that burned in the past, the brick shell is original, but the interior has been rebuilt). However, when Colonial Williamsburg secured the rights to the building, they promptly removed the columns and restored it to its eighteenth-century appearance.

African-American slave standing trial, or perhaps a judge, a jurist, a lawyer, a defendant on trial, or even a Confederate soldier who died there. I chose the word "defendants" quite carefully for this section because when you look at all the apparitions in the courthouse windows, they all have a common theme—they all look angry! Perhaps they were defendants in this court who are still angry over the resulting sentence—or perhaps they are angry for being pronounced guilty when they were innocent. On the next few pages you will find that the paranormal is quite the norm for this original eighteenth-century building.

Ghosts of Defendants?

But when you look in the windows of this building, you can sometimes see the faces of souls that were part of its history: like an

The front of the courthouse; notice the apparition to the right of the cupola. But you want to see the faces in the windows, right?

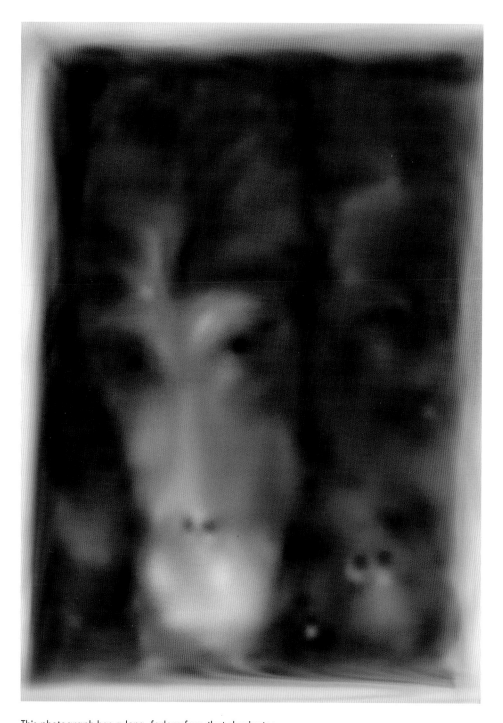

This photograph has a long, forlorn face that dominates the window with a missing mouth (symbolic of something?), joined by what appears to be a bald man with a beard and the smallest face looking like a cross between a man and a pig.

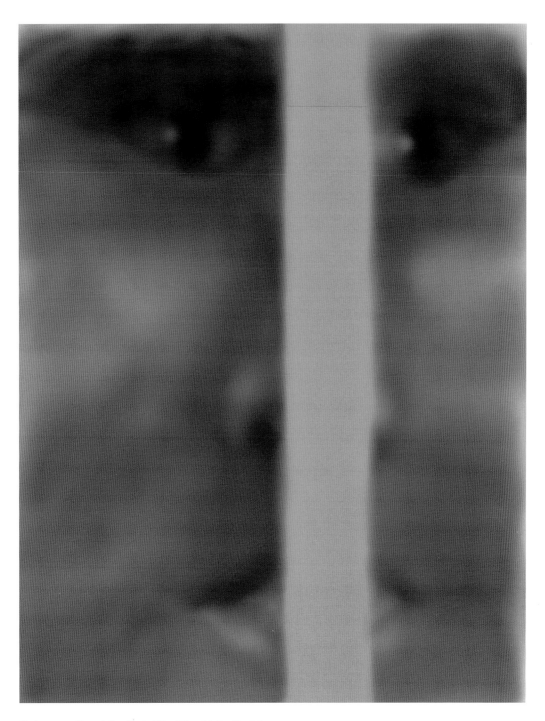

Perhaps another defendant still gritting his teeth at the
verdict he heard in this building?

Could this be one of the defendants who was tried for some crime in this building? The rather dark eyes project a sinister countenance . . .

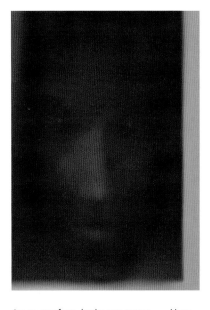

An angry face looks out at me . . . How many people's lives are still connected to this courthouse?

Finally, an African American man, perhaps a runaway slave, appears next to a column of partial white faces; we will take a closer look at this phenomenon in chapter eleven: The white pillar— stay tuned.

THE STOCKS, THE PILLORY, AND THE WHIPPING POST

Cruel, Corporal, and Entertaining?

I know—it's not a building, it's not original, and it doesn't take up much space, but when you see the paranormal activity right around this site, right next to the courthouse, you will understand why I made this a separate chapter. From time to time, I will eliminate sites that have rumors of hauntings that end up lacking compelling stories, history, and photos (in this case, the Nicolson Store) and replace them with something more thought-provoking, if not downright fascinating. The only problem is that without a building with windows, it's hard to get photographs with any great detail, especially in the face. But even so, I believe you will find these photographs compelling— even without facial detail, due to their proximity to tourists. If you have been to this site, then no doubt you have been up close and personal with ghosts, whether you've realized it or not. In fact, at the end of the text part of this chapter, I will tell you how you might get your own photo with a ghost, if you are intrepid enough; old "Blue Face" tries to get in on as many photos as he can . . .

First, let's briefly look at crime and eighteenth-century punishment, so that you can see what a different world it is that we live in from the times of the founding fathers of this country. Punishment was corporal, and there were no prisons to hold criminals. You're thinking, wait a minute—Williamsburg has a jail, spelled *gaol* in the eighteenth century. The jail was used just to hold the accused until they appeared before the court, but of course there were always exceptions: Political prisoners and high-ranking prisoners of war might be kept in the jail. The only other offense a man might find himself spending an indefinite period of time in jail was if he was deemed unable to pay off his debts. The obvious conundrum is how could anyone pay off their debts if they were incarcerated? Some of the founding fathers realized the unfairness of such laws, but it took the government until 1830 to eliminate debtor's prisons.

The most common form of punishment was to fine a person found guilty of a misdemeanor, and the currency used in Virginia was tobacco, so your fine would be in pounds of tobacco. Second to that was a public whipping, with the hands shackled to the post to the far right of the courthouse. This punishment was both public (to humiliate) and painful; the judge would stipulate that the blows, or "stripes," must be "well laid on"— in other words, they could not be whipped lightly. One minor church official, called a beadle, was himself whipped by the sheriff for striking those convicted too lightly. Usually, if a fine did not work with an individual for the first couple of misdemeanors, a public flogging was thought to do the trick.

Next to the whipping post you will find the stocks, a place where you were seated on an uncomfortable, pointed board while your legs were locked in irons. Most of the time, this punishment was carried out on those who were drunk in public (a drunk tank), or sometimes on an enraged individual in order to cool down. Besides the discomfort of time in the stocks, consider this: There were no bathroom breaks, and the public was permitted, if not encouraged, to throw garbage on you.

Closest to the courthouse you will find the pillory, a place where the hands and the head of an individual were secured for discomfort and public shaming. (Many people get the stocks and the pillory mixed up, and some incorrectly call the stocks the stockade, which is a fort. Just remember this: You put your stocking feet into the stocks—the socks into the stocks—and your head goes on a pillow and into the pillory.) Thousands of people that visit Colonial Williamsburg each year have their photo taken while in the pillory, but what they fail to realize is that your earlobes would have been nailed into the wood! What happened when your sentence, usually about two hours, was over? Your earlobes would be slit to remove your head if the deputy felt sorry for you; otherwise your head was just yanked out of the pillory, permanently ripping your ears. Of course, some punishments included the removal of the whole ear. Some of the crimes that were punished by time in the pillory included treason, sedition, arson, blasphemy, witchcraft, perjury, wife beating, cheating, forgery, coin clipping, dice cogging, slandering, conjuring, fortune-telling, and drunkenness, among other offenses. Like the stocks, the crowds were allowed to throw garbage and other things at the person sentenced to the pillory. In some cases, overenthusiastic crowds have pelted the individual to death.

Keep in mind that in the eighteenth century, this courthouse sat in the middle of Market Square, and every family in Williamsburg would come to buy their food for the day each and every day—there were no refrigerators or freezers to keep food fresh. People knew when court was in session, and they would come to the square not only to buy their food, but also to watch miscreants be punished for

their crimes: This was eighteenth-century entertainment. Other punishments that took place in front of the courthouse included the public branding of individuals with hot irons, sometimes on the hand and sometimes on the forehead, the letter chosen to fit the crime. For example, the letter M was chosen for "manslaughter," the letter B chosen for "burglary"; you can see examples of the branding irons at the Williamsburg Gaol, where the interpreters will explain to you more particulars about eighteenth-century crime and punishment.

I have only touched the surface of some of the corporal punishments of the eighteenth century, and the seventeenth century (the 1600s) is even worse. The colonists at Jamestown were subject to what they called "Tyrannycall Lawes written in blood" (seventeenth-century spelling), which included hanging starving men for stealing food, or tying them to a tree and letting them starve to death, burning men to death, working as slaves for years for petty crimes, and breaking men on the wheel, a particularly painful and gruesome form of capital punishment: In the most common way (there are several variations), a man was tied to a large wheel, with his arms and legs between the spokes. The wheel was spun slowly, and the executioner would use a heavy hammer to break the bones in the limbs. After bludgeoning the victim, the condemned man would be left to die on the wheel—sometimes taking three to four days for the onset of death, all the while allowing the birds to feed on the condemned man's still-living body. In comparison to Jamestown, the punishments given out at the pillory, the stocks, and the whipping post seem mild by comparison, but brutal when compared to modern penal codes.

Sometimes we use sayings that come from the eighteenth century, but we have no clue about their origin. For example, one misdemeanor that you could be fined or punished for here is the "rule of thumb." Today, we take for granted that it means an unwritten rule that most people know and follow, but in the 1700s the *rule of thumb* meant that you could beat your wife if she was insubordinate—but not with a stick that was larger in diameter than your thumb. People will sometimes say that a person is branded for life, meaning that an action or mistake that they made will follow them for the rest of their life—a metaphor. Back then the branding was real—and sometimes quite obvious—as mentioned earlier, some misdemeanors would earn you a brand right on the forehead. Most brands were on the hand; but can you imagine forever trying to conceal your hand from onlookers, lest they learn what crime you have been convicted of?

Now that you are familiar with what went on just outside the Courthouse of 1770, is it any wonder that the paranormal activity is so high? Even with modern crime detection techniques, I have watched, heard, and read about the stories of men who were falsely accused and incarcerated for years, if not almost a whole lifetime, for crimes they did not commit; it gives me pause to wonder how many men were falsely accused and punished here. (Note that no one was executed here, sentencing a man to death was only done at the Capitol and the executions were carried out down Capitol Landing Road.) Keep in mind too that during the Battle of Williamsburg (Civil War—May 5, 1862) this courthouse was used as a hospital for the wounded and dying, with a mass grave nearby—another possible reason for the ghosts.

Old Blue Face, the Tourist Family, and the Bodybuilder

Quite a few years ago someone in my family had their photo taken at the pillory; when the photo was developed there was a ghostly face that appeared over his. Recalling that, when I began writing these books I inquired about the whereabouts of the photo—but it seems to be lost. I figured that if it could happen once, I could make it happen again. I began to take a lot of photos in and around the pillory, and I discovered one ghost that tried to be a part of each and almost every photograph: Old Blue Face. He (or she?) especially likes to appear when there are children around—sometimes with a few of his (or her) friends. I don't know the ghost's connection to the pillory, but it is his or her preferred hangout.

I next discovered what appears to be a tourist family; I have a compelling photo of a man in blue jeans crossing the street, and what appears to be a family (a wife and two kids) waiting for him. I know, it seems difficult to juxtapose a modern tourist family next to all of these Revolutionary and Civil War characters, but I guess they are all sharing the same dimensions.

I have also seen the ephemeral outline of a fellow that may be a bodybuilder. Although I can never get the face of a ghost on the street as clearly as I can in the window of a house, these photographs prove that not all ghosts are confined to a particular house or building. However, what I do not know is how far they can roam the streets; perhaps the rules are different for them.

Something else that you may discover on an evening walk through Colonial Williamsburg: If you happen to try out the pillory or the stocks (at the front right side of the courthouse), and you have your photo taken by someone else, don't be surprised if you see an orb or even another face over your own—it happens quite often! Try it—you might be unpleasantly surprised! It might be Old Blue Face, one of the tourist family, the bodybuilder, or even a Confederate soldier!

Check out the photos of the phantoms that lurk around the pillory, the stocks, and the whipping post. Perhaps you will meet one of them if you have your photo taken there, or maybe you will just see the marching feet of soldiers that no longer have bodies . . .

Here's the pillory, just outside the Courthouse of 1770, where someone convicted of a misdemeanor would place their head and hands; keep in mind that part of the punishment is that they would nail your earlobes to the wood! Once placed there, anyone was free to pelt the trapped person with whatever they could throw—eggs and rotten fruit were a crowd favorite, but they could also throw rocks!

Old Blue Face makes one of his (or her) appearances with a group of kids at the pillory.

Old Blue Face shows up again with some of his friends at the pillory, anxious to get in the photo with an unidentified middle-school boy, whose face I have blurred.

Old Blue Face and friends, this time with a face that's unusually dark, and perhaps a little foreboding. The ghosts have just about blocked out the young boy standing with his head in the pillory.

In this photo, Blue Face and the dark face show up again, this time completely covering the face of one of the teachers who brought the group of middle-schoolers to Williamsburg. Still want to get your photo taken at the pillory? Try waiting till dusk . . .

This odd coupling of ghosts includes two faces, a torso that is much too small to go with either face, and a pair of legs that do not go with any of the above—right in front of the pillory by the Courthouse of 1770 steps.

Here is the partially visible ghost of a man who looks like a bodybuilder, standing right on the street in front of the pillory. Do you see another ghost trying to appear on his chest?

Here you can see the tourist family: A man in blue jeans and a black belt with possibly a camera strap across one shoulder walks towards what may be his family—a woman in a blue-striped skirt with two children (the child to the left is barely visible except for his legs). You can see the end of the pillory and the legs of two real persons standing to the right.

Here are four disembodied legs that seemed to show up in almost every photograph one night between the pillory and the Courthouse of 1770. Where does this fit on your scale of the weird?

ANOMALY IN THE WINDOWS

The White Pillar

As I said in the first book, every time I come across a new type of apparition or a new face, I want to document it and share it. The last photograph of the face in the courthouse window was the segue into this chapter, not only showing an African-American face but also a bright-white pillar of light. You have seen the ghostly white faces that resemble the *classic white* type of Halloween ghost: A bright white appearance with darkened areas for the eyes, sometimes a mouth, and even less frequently with a nose feature. I have seen these types of apparitions most frequently at the jail and at the slaves' quarters (do you remember from the first book?). Lately I've been finding something that looks like a bright white pillar of light. Obviously there is no source for the light, and the pillar has minimal or is devoid of any facial features. When I take a photo of a house or building, these white pillars stand out even without magnification or upping the contrast in the photo. If you looked closely at the last photograph from the courthouse, you will see no discernible facial features; perhaps some are trying to form, but it really does not resemble a face.

The more experienced I become with paranormal photography, the more convinced I am that making a visual appearance for people to see or the camera to photograph is something that ghosts learn how to do— *otherwise they would all be doing it.* But I only see the faces or partial faces in some homes, whereas other apparitions only appear above the house or building that they occupy or haunt as red super cells or as spherical torches. People love to be recognized, and in my line of rational thought how much more so would an entity that is stuck in some sort of hellish limbo for possibly centuries want to be recognized and, yes, even helped. Unless they dwell between dimensions, and are able to do things in a dimension we cannot see, from all apparent appearances these creatures have nothing to do but hover over the house or building that keeps them here for who knows how long.

The first photograph from this chapter is from the jail, and it is somewhere between a featureless white pillar and a classic Halloween type with facial features—perhaps eyespots and possibly a frown. The second photo is from the Lightfoot House (on the Duke of Gloucester Street—yes, there are two Lightfoot Houses in Colonial Williamsburg!), and it is pretty much featureless—the classic white pillar. The third photo is sitting on the windowsill of the Powder Magazine, and it appears to have one eye. The fourth photo likewise only has one eye, albeit better defined; this photo was taken at the Tayloe House, an original eighteenth-century home of a Loyalist to the crown whose backyard woods was full of American (Continental) soldiers. Noise from the encampments behind this home has been heard by many tourists as well as employees of Colonial Williamsburg. The noise includes music and sounds of celebration— perhaps of the victory at Yorktown. Could the apparition be Colonel Tayloe himself, a Loyalist to the English crown who may have been more than a little nervous about the soldiers camped in his backyard—after all, in their eyes Tayloe was a traitor! Finally, the last photo is from the always reliable and notorious Peyton Randolph House—a place where I can readily go to find some bizarre apparition or an intimidating pair of eyes. Yes, even the white pillar takes on an unusual, bizarre appearance at the Randolph House— and again it lives up to its infamous reputation. Compare the photographs on the following pages to the photo from the jail from Part I, which does have facial features:

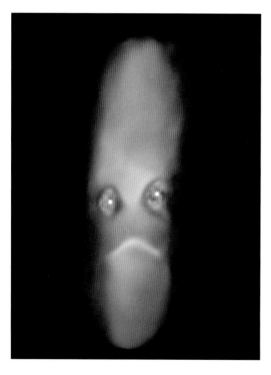

This white pillar is from the jail, perhaps with eyespots and a frown.

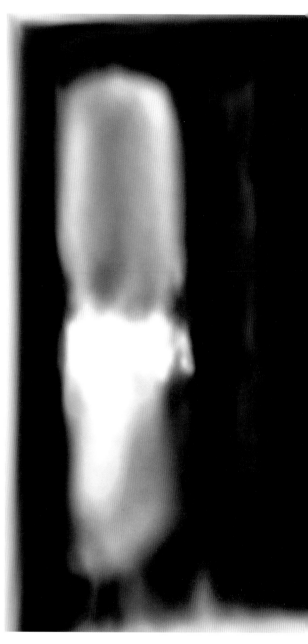

A white pillar from the Lightfoot House on the Duke of Gloucester St. (Yes, there are two Lightfoot Houses.)

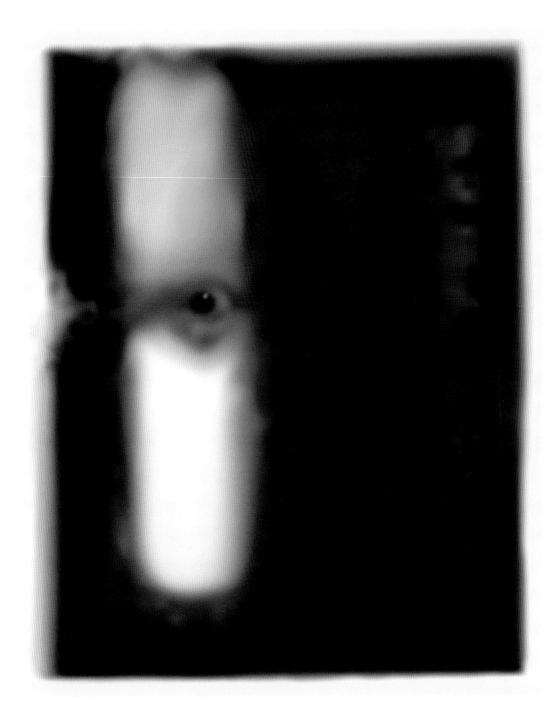

This white pillar has a more human-looking eye than most; this photo was taken at the Tayloe House, an original eighteenth-century house owned by a man who was a Loyalist to the crown, and yet he had American (Continental) soldiers camped in his backwoods yard.

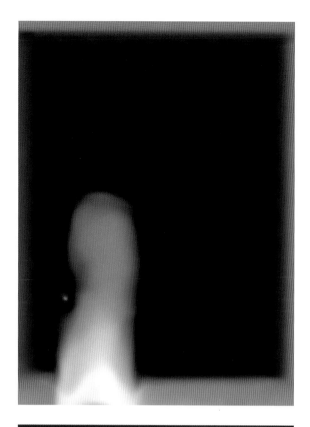

A white pillar from the powder magazine, with one eyespot; notice that it is outside the window and extends below it.

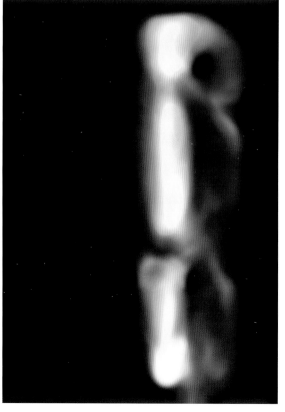

This is the most bizarre of the white pillars (par for the Peyton Randolph House), and I was not going to use it until they started to show up in the windows of other homes, so I picked the most interesting ones to place in a chapter about this new kind of apparition.

THE POWDER MAGAZINE

*The Phantom Militia—The Largest Group of
Ghosts Ever Caught on Camera?*

History

Governor Spotswood had the powder magazine built in 1715, as a storehouse for the Virginia militia to defend itself against aggressors—which at that point in time was mainly attacks from Native Americans as more and more of them were displaced from their ancestral lands. Other threats to the Colony of Virginia included riots, revolts (like Bacon's Rebellion), slave revolts, and pirates. During the period of the French and Indian War (1754–1763), Virginia supported large-scale military operations, and the magazine provided storage for armaments and supplies (guns, shot, kegs of powder, flints, tents, tools, swords, pikes, canteens, cooking utensils, and flintlocks). The governor ordered the guardhouse to be built as well as a high wall around the magazine because so many weapons and supplies to fight the war were coming through Williamsburg and being stored at the magazine until they were shipped off to the British-American units needing them. Both the original wall and the original guardhouse were pulled down in the nineteenth century, and both have been rebuilt with the aid of archeology, sketches, and engravings that showed their appearance.

What many people don't realize is that the day after the Battles of Lexington and Concord, Virginia's Governor Dunmore ordered British troops in Virginia to do the same thing that preempted the opening battles of the Revolutionary War by Massachusetts Governor Gage: Seize the gunpowder stores at the magazine. But Dunmore made a threat to Virginians that they did not take lightly: If any Virginians took up arms against the crown and any British official was harmed, he would "declare freedom to the slaves and reduce the City of Williamsburg to ashes." In other words, any slave who wanted freedom could be granted it if they took up arms for the crown. In the 1760s, slave rebellions were common—so this was a viable threat—not to mention that the whole southern economy depended on slave labor and would be disrupted, so Virginians were more cautious than their counterparts in Massachusetts.

In the end, the British soldiers got away with fifteen half barrels of gunpowder before citizens in Williamsburg discovered the theft and sounded the alarms (drumbeats). An angry mob gathered and was ready to storm the governor's palace to get Dunmore, but several men, including Peyton Randolph, asked for calmer heads to prevail and send a delegation to Dunmore to demand explanation. Patrick Henry marched 150 militiamen to Williamsburg to demand the gunpowder be returned; but one plantation owner decided to pay for the powder to avoid conflict. About one month later, two young men were seriously injured when they broke into the magazine and were shot by a spring-gun trap (opening the door triggered the gun to fire), arousing an angry mob to storm the building and take it over one day later. The records do not say if these two young men died or not, but I find it interesting that I was able to capture the faces of two young men at the powder magazine—one in the window and one at the wall.

Another fact that many do not know is that Virginia Governor Dunmore was accused of using biological warfare during the Revolutionary War. Lord Dunmore eventually made good on his threat to issue an Emancipation Proclamation for any slave who would fight for the crown as well as declaring martial law on November 25, 1775. Historians estimate that about 1,000 men took Dunmore up on his offer, and they were used to make raids in Virginia. But he also gave these men blankets used to cover victims of smallpox—a deadly disease in eighteenth-century America—and sent them out into the Virginia countryside in hopes of starting an epidemic. Biological warfare backfired on Dunmore, because he lost most of this slave force to the disease with little effect on the population in Virginia. As a consequence, Dunmore became what some label as the first American villain, and perhaps the first to use biological weapons in North America.

When Thomas Jefferson moved the capital of Virginia to Richmond, the powder magazine ceased to be used as a storage facility for armaments and went through a variety of uses before going full circle and returning to its original storage function as part of Colonial Williamsburg's living museum. Some of the octagonal building's later uses include the following: a market, Baptist meetinghouse, Confederate arsenal, dancing school, and livery stable.

The Children and the Ghost Militia

I have photographed the grounds surrounding the powder magazine many times and have captured nothing paranormal—but one evening a group of children were on the green and everything changed, solidifying the idea (at least from my experience) that ghosts are attracted to youth. In the magazine you saw in the previous chapter an apparition that I capture periodically in one of the windowpanes of the powder magazine—a white pillar of light, sometimes with and sometimes without an eyespot. It usually is on the outside of the upstairs windowpane, because you can see the white light below the windowsill. Another ghostly face regularly appears on the other side of the magazine—particularly when there is a military demonstration on the grounds in front and to the side of the magazine (part of Market Square).

Although there may be endless possibilities for the hauntings of the powder magazine and its grounds, I am inclined to think it has to do with a Civil War mass gravesite that you will read about in the next chapter that was located somewhere nearby. But there is an outdoor activity that seems to bring out all of the ghosts from the Revolutionary War as well.

One evening, Colonial Williamsburg was training some middle-schoolers to be in the Virginia militia. They were taught military drills, including how to march, how to carry their weapons, and other commands that every trained eighteenth-century soldier would have to know. Immediately after the drills finished, I captured the area in a photograph, and the ghosts that are usually invisible around the magazine were out and apparently observing the military proceedings.

I was excited about finding gigantic apparitions over and around the magazine. There were three of Colonial Williamsburg's militia-men standing at attention at the ceremony's beginning, and I photographed them from the back—they were completely surrounded by an unknown number of apparitions that were evidently interested in participating in the military proceedings.

But when I got home and was able to see the photographs at full resolution, I discovered the real coup de grace: Standing at the wall on the left was an ephemeral group of figures in military order. As I took a closer look, I discovered that I had photographed a whole ghost militia! I have never captured that many ghosts in one place—but even though they are not as clear as I would have liked, you can make out in the close-up what appears to be men lined up at the wall in eighteenth-century uniforms. (The determining factor is the bandoleers across the front of some of their uniforms.) Some former Colonial Williamsburg interpreters have even suggested that this is the group of British soldiers sent to steal the gunpowder from the magazine. Whether they are British soldiers or Virginia militiamen, they are the largest group of ghosts that I (or possibly anyone else?) has ever taken in a photograph. A few minutes later I discovered that all of the phantom soldiers joined the middle-schoolers as they performed military drills, standing around them as if they were a part of the training.

Next I found a group of females in eighteenth-century attire walking across the field in front of the magazine, and in the following photograph a single woman who streaked across the field as if she wanted to be a part of the next photo—once again demonstrating just how fast ghosts can move!

The photographs in this chapter were a profound moment of discovery as I realized that it is possible for ghosts to gather in large groups as well as a seeming desire to interact with children!

The Magazine on a paranormal night; the soldiers that you see standing to the left are real, or should I say alive—unlike what is coming up.

Perhaps you were not impressed with the previous photo; how about several ghost soldiers? The soldiers on the right are real (although there are two bright orbs on the drummer) and the three soldiers on the left are ghosts. Did you notice the outline of either a gun or a walking stick?

This is one of my most amazing finds ever! In this photo, besides the huge apparitions over the Magazine, if you look along the wall on the left, you can see what appears to be a ghost militia.

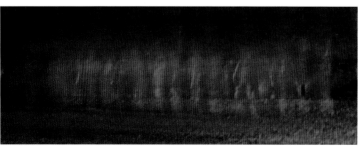

Here is a close-up of the phantom foot soldiers.

Exactly two weeks after the first photo of the ghost militia, I captured them again—this time marching from the left side to the door of the Powder Magazine. I was thrilled about this photograph because it was an affirmation about the first and not just a one-time fluke. I don't know if it's possible, but I hope to get a clearer, more defined photo in the future.

Here is a second close-up of the ghost militia.

Even more amazing—on that same night I captured the ghosts standing next to a group of middle-school students that were being trained by Colonial Williamsburg's reenactors to be in the Virginia Militia.

Here is a close-up, where you can see that some of the ghosts are quite tall.

When I took this photo, I was hoping for a closer capture of the ghost militia. But instead, notice the streaking apparitions right in front of the middle-school class.

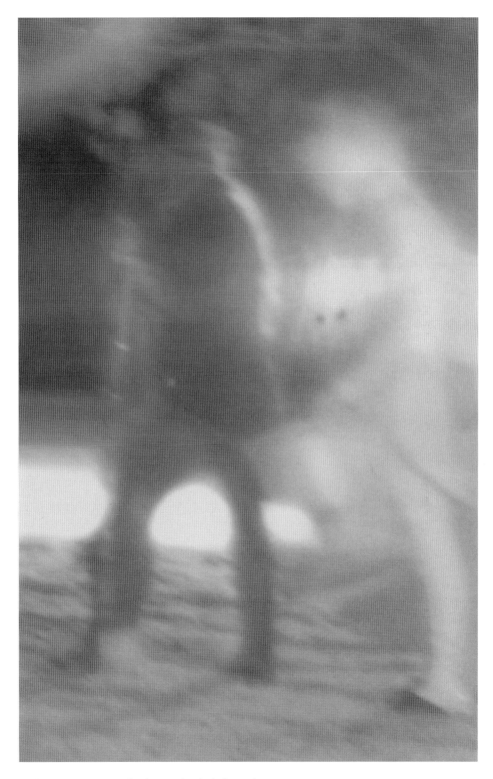

A ghost . . . or two are shadowing the dark-figured
Colonial Williamsburg militiaman.

Members of the ghost militia (the bright white figures) surround several middle-school students (the dark figures).

This close-up is a figure of a woman who seems to be streaking to the spot, so much so that her hair seems to be flying in the wind. In a photograph a second later she disappeared.

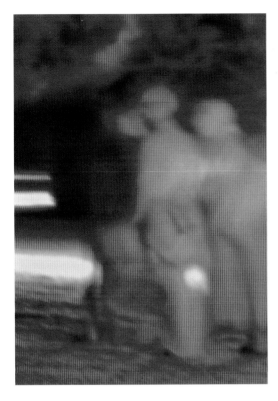

I expected to see only soldiers in front of the Powder Magazine, but this area also doubled as a marketplace for local farmers and fishermen. If you look at the figures closely, you see dresses and fabric caps worn by women in the eighteenth century—going to the farmer's market.

This apparition showed up at the wall around the magazine—a very transparent face—with several other faces around it trying to show up.

Here is one of the occupants of the Powder Magazine (the other appears as a one-eyed white pillar seen earlier). Could this be one of the teenage boys who fell victim to the British booby-trap, or is it someone older?

THE MARKET SQUARE TAVERN

Jefferson . . . and Perhaps the Yankee Butcher?

History

Market Square was a plot of land established in the original town plan of 1699, to create a type of farmer's market for daily provisions needed by the townspeople. In the eighteenth century refrigerators, freezers, packaging, and preservatives (except for the salt that was placed on meats) were nonexistent, and so each family in the town would have to go shopping *daily* for the food they would consume. Farmers would sell their produce from a cart, as well as provisions such as eggs, milk, and butter. Fishermen would also sell the food they caught in the nearby York and James Rivers: a variety of fish and shellfish, including oysters that were as big as dinner plates (try finding that today!). On certain days contests would be held, such as foot races, dancing, "exercises," and chasing after a pig with a soaped tail, with prizes offered to the winners of each contest. The Market Square tavern stood next to a hub of activity each and every day.

John Dixon leased the land right next to the market square in 1749, from the city of Williamsburg, probably starting out with a small building that would later either be enlarged or torn down and rebuilt. The lease passed through a number of hands, and sometime between 1749 and 1760, a building of great value was erected here. Gabriel Maupin, a French Huguenot, bought the tavern in September of 1771. Maupin was the keeper of the powder magazine that was right next

door to him, and stood solidly with the American cause against the English crown. (I'm sure that the fact that he was French also had something to do with it, considering the acerbic relationship between the two countries for hundreds of years.) It has always been a popular trend to name children after popular culture heroes, and the vogue starting in 1775, was to name your son after George Washington; hence we have George Washington Maupin born that year to the proud father and owner of the Market Square Tavern.

Keeping a tavern in the war-torn area of Williamsburg was difficult, because soldiers quartered in Williamsburg or in any of the camps in the surrounding James City County would often impress (take for the use of war) the horses in the tavern pastures. He would often advertise for these "strayed or stolen" horses until, in January of 1776, he announced he would no longer be responsible for them. Most people today have no clue what the ravages of war can do to both family and business.

Rather than bore you with a long list of owners of the tavern, I want to mention the Market Square Tavern's most famous resident: Thomas Jefferson. Jefferson first came to Williamsburg in 1760, to attend the College of William and Mary. After he finished his studies (he did not graduate though), he came under the tutelage of George Wythe for law, and during these studies, Jefferson was a resident of the Market Square Tavern. Jefferson is one of the familiar names that put Williamsburg on the map for most Americans, and he was the person who took Williamsburg off the map by moving the capital to Richmond—essentially putting Williamsburg back into obscurity until it became a living history museum. (Jefferson said that he felt Williamsburg was susceptible to naval bombardment from the British navy via College Creek, which connects to the James River, and he felt the capitol would be safer in Richmond—and closer to his home!) Williamsburg, the bustling capital, became a sleepy small town in the rural South, preserving all of the eighteenth-century buildings for posterity, including the Market Square Tavern, and preserving their paranormal occupants for you to see.

Soldiers Searching for Their Limbs . . . and the Yankee Butcher

Many sightings of ghosts at the Market Square Tavern are of Confederate soldiers. Somewhere on the grounds of the tavern a church had been built, and during the Civil War, the Confederate army used it as a hospital (the Battle of Williamsburg or the Battle of Fort Magruder, whichever you prefer to call it). Although the church has disappeared long ago, what hasn't is a mass grave with more than 200 bodies—and an amputation pit filled with the shattered arms and legs of soldiers wounded in battle. (Do you remember another large house in Colonial Williamsburg with an eerily similar story—from the first book?) What is hard to imagine is the scope of the dead and wounded from that battle; keep in mind that the Civil War was fought like an old-style European battle, with lines of men marching up and shooting each other—often just a short distance apart—and that's a recipe for carnage. According to the Civil War Trust, close to 73,000 men fought, and 3,843 men

died in this battle, with countless others wounded.[1] A mass grave of 200 is just a drop in the bucket in comparison to the almost 4,000 men who lost their lives, and it begs the question, "How many more mass graves are in Williamsburg that have no markers?"

Some guests who have stayed at the Market Square Tavern have witnessed a Confederate soldier with an arm missing, digging in the ground—searching for the amputation pit that holds his missing arm? Others have seen wounded Confederate soldiers roaming the area, and some have heard the screams of pain coming out of nowhere; perhaps another soldier enduring the agony of losing an arm or a leg without anesthetic is suspended in time, reliving the agony over and over. One night in particular, it seemed that all the guests were awakened by the sound of digging, and called to the front desk to report it. The problem was there was no digging going on—no construction happening during the night! One couple looked out the window to report seeing a woman in a long dress placing a flower on the ground—on the site that they would later find out to be a mass grave of Confederate soldiers. After the woman laid down the flower, she disappeared . . .

Some say that they have seen Thomas Jefferson in the tavern, but I have no verified accounts of that. There is one story pertaining to Jefferson and his former accommodations as a law student that began with a skeptic announcing to his companions that he did not believe in hauntings and that the ghost of Thomas Jefferson could not possibly be there. Immediately the curtains began to blow violently, and they felt the temperature in the room drop considerably, but there was no wind! The small group could see that there were no open doors or windows to account for the movement of the curtains or the drop in temperature. So no, I can't say for sure that

Thomas Jefferson haunts the Market Square Tavern, but I can say that a wraith wanted the skeptic to know that the paranormal was real.

After the Confederate retreat to Richmond, the Union troops were stationed in Williamsburg, the point of demarcation between territory held by the Union army and a sort of no-man's-land between here and Richmond—the Union tried to advance on Richmond after the Battle in Williamsburg, but were soundly defeated by the Confederates. Back here in Williamsburg, the head surgeon for the Union was not only an alcoholic, but he was also a butcher—earning this reputation and moniker because he needlessly amputated arms and legs that could have been saved. How many of these Union and Confederate phantoms died from an infection as a result of one of the butcher's unnecessary amputations? Perhaps if you see one, you can inquire if he is one of the victims of the Yankee butcher . . .

Can you imagine being on this property on May 5 and 6, 1862, and hearing the screams of pain as a soldier's arms and legs are sawn off with no anesthetic? Can you imagine seeing piles of arms and legs, with more being brought out every few minutes and cast upon the pile? Some of those dead soldiers' spirits are still here. For example, four faces happened to show up in the front window when a rather noisy ghost tour gathered together around their tour guide just a few feet away from me. They all came to the window to look just as I pressed the shutter button! Some showed up in the upstairs windows, and others showed up in the back of the tavern; the final one showed up in the trees, and is wearing what may be the cap of a Confederate soldier. Market Square Tavern hosts a plethora of guests—both living and dead!

A dominant spherical torch looms overhead, along with a whole array of characters to be seen.

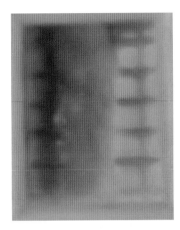
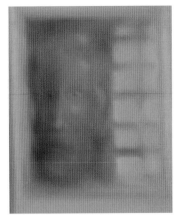
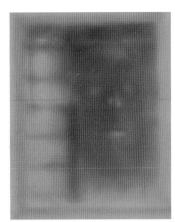

Although Thomas Jefferson stayed in this original building while attending William and Mary, the ghosts are not likely him, but four of the many Confederate soldiers who lost their lives in a makeshift hospital that was a church on the grounds of the Market Square Tavern. This group came out to look at a ghost tour that gathered a few feet behind me.

This final face was floating on the Market Square Green next to the tavern. The cap seems to resemble the kind used with the Confederate uniform—a former Rebel soldier?

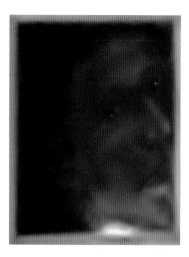

This group of faces made an appearance in the tavern's dark windows around the back of the building.

THE RALEIGH TAVERN

Whatever Happened to Blackbeard's Skull?

History

The Raleigh Tavern began its role as the place to go for Virginia's elite circa 1717, its proximity to the Capitol building being key to the role it played in the lives of those who governed the colony and to all of the lawyers, plaintiffs, and defendants who were a part of any legal proceeding in Virginia. (It was named after Sir Walter Raleigh, the man who recruited 117 men, women, and children to establish the first English colony here in America on Roanoke Island, in 1587, twenty years before Jamestown—but it would disappear without a trace.) The Raleigh Tavern was popular, and the "Apollo Room" was where the elegant balls, dancing, feasting, and yes, gambling took place for the movers and shakers in Virginia and later American politics.

Even more important than all of the partying done by Virginia's rich and famous, was the Raleigh's role as the colony's alternate Capitol when the governor dissolved the House of Burgesses. The first time this took place was in 1769, when Lord Botetourt dissolved the legislative body because of their protesting the Townsend Acts. Rather than accepting the governor's ruling, the more intrepid legislators reconvened at the Raleigh Tavern, agreeing to a nonimportation association, which essentially boycotted certain goods from British merchants. In 1773, a secret meeting was held in a private room at the Raleigh to create a line of communication between all of the colonies: The likes of Thomas Jefferson and Patrick Henry (among others) put together a Committee of Correspondence that was the first step in unifying all of the colonies against something they were dead set against—taxation without representation. A new royal governor, Dunmore, again dissolved the House of Burgesses when they protested the sanction against the port of Boston after the "Tea Party." This time eighty-nine burgesses met at the Raleigh to create another agreement to boycott British goods; a pair of Georges were integrally involved in the process—George Mason drafted it, and George Washington introduced it.

Besides its role as a pseudo-capitol, the Raleigh Tavern was where the Phi Beta Kappa Society was created in 1776, by a group of William and Mary students. The year 1779 saw the creation of what may be the oldest men's social organization in the country: the Pulaski Club, which still is in existence and still meets today. The Raleigh was the site of balls and celebrations for the elite, including Governor Botetourt's first night in Williamsburg and Peyton Randolph's triumphant return from Philadelphia as president of the First Continental Congress. A celebration, which began with Benjamin Waller reading the news of the treaty ending the Revolutionary War, ended at the Raleigh. Another noteworthy celebration was the return of General Lafayette to America, in 1824, to see how the democracy that he fought for was faring. On the negative side of things, merchandise as well as slaves were auctioned off on the steps of the Raleigh Tavern. The original Raleigh Tavern burned down in 1859; according to a Richmond newspaper, it was at the hands of an arsonist.

Another point of interest about the Raleigh Tavern is that it had a punch bowl with a very storied past. After Blackbeard the pirate was killed by a crewman from the ship of Captain Maynard (1718), his head was cut off and placed on a pike at the confluence of the James and Hampton Rivers, known as Blackbeard's Point. But publisher John F. Watson states that the "skull was made into the bottom part of a very large punch bowl, called the infant, which was long used as a drinking vessel at the Raleigh Tavern in Williamsburg. It was enlarged with silver, or silver plated, and I have seen those whose forefathers have spoken of their drinking punch from it . . ." Of course, that punch was laden with a pirate's favorite drink—rum. There has long been something about drinking from the skull of your vanquished enemy, and Blackbeard was larger than life as an infamous foe of Virginia's elite—hence they gathered at the Raleigh to celebrate their accomplishments with this relic from Virginia's storied past.[1]

The Wizards of Williamsburg, the Scents, the Smells, and the Skull

So at the Raleigh Tavern, we have appearances by George Washington, Thomas Jefferson, Patrick Henry, George Mason, Peyton Randolph—giants in the formation of the fledgling democracy, as well as the posthumous appearance of Blackbeard. But since these men all died elsewhere, who are the ghosts? Although Henry Whetherburn ran the Raleigh for a while, the untimely death of his wife after his discovery that she had hidden away a cache of money occurred later when he owned his own tavern. So there are no notable

deaths or suicides at the Raleigh that would explain the presence of ghosts, but they are there nonetheless, with reports all the way back into the nineteenth century! I have since found out that ghosts will return to places that they enjoyed in life—and so some of those larger-than-life figures may haunt the Raleigh regardless of their location at the time of death.

From all the way back in 1856, when Samuel Armistead was brave enough to step forward and tell the story of his paranormal encounter, until today, tourists and Colonial Williamsburg employees alike have all told a similar story about the Raleigh Tavern: They are walking down the Duke of Gloucester on the north side heading towards the Capitol. As they get closer and closer to the Raleigh Tavern, they hear a party going on—music, laughter, and the sounds of a lot of people talking. They also smell the scent of "sweet" tobacco, not the smell of modern cigarettes but a more pleasant smell—but tobacco nonetheless. Their ears tell them that the sounds are coming from the direction of the Raleigh, and as they approach the building, the sounds get louder and louder. But there was only one problem: The tavern was in darkness—not even one light on. For each person who has experienced this series of events, all of the stories end with the same action. The person looks inside one of the windows of the tavern to not only see the rooms in darkness, but it's as if a switch is turned off at that moment. All of the music and laughter ceases, and tobacco smoke no longer permeates the air, leaving the witness to the sounds and smells of the eighteenth century a bit confused as to what just happened.

I have a question for you: Do the ghosts really duplicate the sounds and smells or just recreate them telepathically in the person's mind as they walk by? Now I have proof that these creatures emit light, so they must be able to manipulate light in order to recreate their faces or even the white pillars in the windows of the homes they haunt. At the Raleigh Tavern, the ghosts prefer to recreate sounds and scents rather than manipulate light to show their former selves. Could this be because there are no artificial lights on (inside or out) at the Raleigh during the night? Do they need a light source to manipulate light?

Even though most, if not all, of the ghost stories associated with the Raleigh Tavern include sound and smell, I have discovered that they are capable of manipulating light to create likenesses of what I assume to be past occupants or owners of the former tavern. After photographing this building many times, I became resigned to the fact that I was not ever going to get any faces at the Raleigh. I decided to give it one more try, and on that one night I seemed to hit the mother lode of ghostly apparitions, as you will soon see. Why? Because someone had left the interior lights on during the night! I could not help but conclude that ghosts need an artificial light source to have the energy and/or ability to manipulate light to look like there former selves. These "light manipulators" created quite an array of characters, several of them heavily bearded and looking very much like pictures of the wizards of old from the days when Celtic nature worship dominated the English countryside. More realistically they were from the nineteenth-century Civil War era when long, full beards were in vogue. One ghost has outstretched arms as if trying to get my attention, and another creates a rather frightening apparition that closely resembles a skull . . . perhaps the skull of a certain pirate?

This is the reconstructed Raleigh Tavern, with two faint red super cells to the top left. These two ghosts prefer to recreate the sounds and smells of the tavern; people have heard eighteenth-century music, talking and laughter, and smelled the "sweet scent of tobacco" while walking by the tavern—and yet see nothing when they look inside the windows.

Can you see a figure and multiple faces in this
window at the Raleigh?

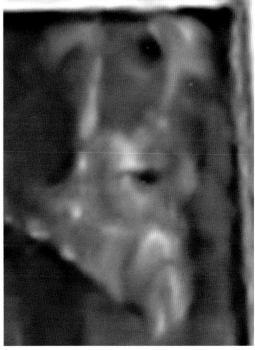

This reminds me of one of those trick photographs that, depending on how you look at it, determines where you see (in this case) a Merlin-like apparition.

Another face—or is it a skull? Blackbeard's skull in the window of the Raleigh Tavern? No, that's not hair, but another wispy apparition with two eyespots at the bottom.

I've read and heard stories of "the woman in white" for years in a lot of different places; I finally found her—in a building that never has had a woman in white legend, and with her arms outstretched—why?

Two different apparitions struggle to appear over
each other.

JOSIAH CHOWNING'S TAVERN

The Phantom Assault

In sharp contrast to the Raleigh Tavern, which catered to the powerful, the rich, and the famous—the "gentry" class of Virginia, Josiah Chowning set up a tavern in 1765, (with its first ad in the *Virginia Gazette*) for the common man on the northeast corner of Market Square and right next to the Courthouse of 1770. Although the property had previously been the sight of many different businesses (and uses), including a blacksmith, a butcher, a merchant, as a rental to a spinster, a merchant, and a wheelwright, Colonial Williamsburg chose to revive the building's role as a tavern to demonstrate how the average Virginian would have eaten, drank, and yes, even gamed. Chowning, who already possessed a 235-acre farm at Powhatan Plantation, must have been looking to supplement his income with the tavern. It was a short-lived venture, lasting from early in 1765 until sometime before April of 1768, when the tavern came under the management of William Elliot—and he only lasted a few months before a wigmaker rented the building.

The most famous resident of this house was John Tyler, a James City County Magistrate, as well as a marshal to the court of admiralty. His son, John Tyler was the executor of his father's will and would sell his father's property in Williamsburg in 1773, as well as father the country's tenth president, John Tyler. Several of Virginia's wealthiest families would keep the first and last name the same from father to son without adding Sr., Jr., or numbers after the names. So our tenth president was really John Tyler IV; Tyler's Charles City neighbors, the Harrisons had a similar story with the name Benjamin and the Byrds with the name William.

Not too long after the Tylers, a man named Graham Frank owned the property, and researchers believe that he was a Loyalist to England during the Revolutionary War, resulting in this property being taken by the state (more properly called a "Commonwealth") of Virginia in 1779. If you recall from the first book, Mad Lucy Ludwell's property had the same fate (called *escheating*) for her partiality to the crown. Loyalty to the crown during the Revolutionary War was a liability that would result in the loss of your property and the contempt of all those around you.

Out of the many owners and renters of this property, these are some of the more interesting. Finally, in 1895, Dr. Samuel Griffin turned the tavern into the Colonial Hotel, and it became a gathering for the courthouse crowd until Colonial Williamsburg acquired the building and tore it down to the original foundations—reconstructing the tavern for the common man of the eighteenth century—and enabling you to sample that lifestyle.

A Paranormal Love and Assault

Chowning's has a lot of paranormal activity in the form of moving and rearranging the tavern furniture. Occasionally, the paranormal activity will reach the harassment level, an example being the experience of one waitress a few years ago. After using the restroom, she had a difficult time getting out. As she would grab the door handle to open it, an unseen force would pull it out of her hand—and the door has no handle on the outside for anyone to grab, because the door just pushes open to enter the bathroom. So the entity kept yanking the door out of the distraught waitress' hands, all the while she realized that a person could not possibly be on the other side because there was nothing to grab on to. The frightened woman was reluctant to ever use the restroom again.

On a completely different note, this ghost story has all of the makings of a paranormal romance—that is if the waitress wasn't so frightened of the possibilities. The ghost of a Confederate soldier found a way to charm the woman of his dreams, a waitress at Chowning's Tavern, when he found an open line of communication via a psychic medium who happened to be dining there that evening. She communicated to the waitress that the young soldier was infatuated with her, and to demonstrate his affection he delivered a large magnolia flower from up the street. To this day no one can explain how the flower arrived at the tavern! I'm sure that a paranormal romance writer would love to take this story and run with it, but the reality is that the waitress could neither see nor talk to her suitor from the previous century, so this budding love story has a tragic ending for the enamored ghost . . .

This last story about Chowning's is the most profound, if not downright frightening, with an added dose of timelessness and helplessness. One evening, when coming from the back street next to Chowning's, two friends (off-duty police officer Chuck Rayle, and his photographer friend, heard a group of what sounded like four to five males and one female

laughing and joking—the sound emanating from the front of the tavern. As the two men walked toward the side of the tavern, the conversation they'd overheard turned hostile and aggressive on the part of the males and alarmed on the part of the lone female. The conversation was not at all muffled, but in the words of the photographer, "Clear as a bell."

Next it sounded like the young woman was being assaulted, and she began to scream "NO!" The police officer was carrying his gun and badge, and so the two began to sprint to round the corner of the tavern. The police officer then did something he had never done before: He put his hand on his sidearm ready to draw it in anticipation of breaking up a gang attack and rape, and his companion got out his cellphone and dialed 911. As the two broke into a run, the photographer said, "Just tell me when to press 'send' and I will!" Seconds later they rounded the corner to the front of Chowning's Tavern to find that there was no one there! Puzzled at the proximity of the voices, they began to frantically look around to see if the group was anywhere nearby. They came up with nothing as they began to realize that they had just heard a moment in time, perhaps playing over and over, and the sinking feeling that they were helpless to do anything but witness the soundtrack of a terrified woman's memory, perhaps paying the ultimate price for being in the wrong place at the wrong time. About a year later, the two were walking down the same street and they heard the water running through the grate, the night insects calling to each other, and a breeze through the trees. They realized that all of that ambient noise was missing the night they heard the phantom assault on the woman; it was as if it was missing . . . was it?

Here is Chowning's Tavern; notice the red super cell on the side. I wonder if that apparition is responsible for recreating the sounds from the assault that you read about?

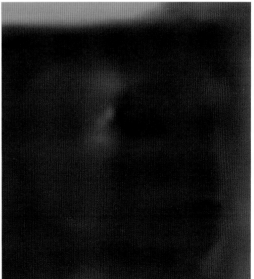

The first two faces that I discovered at Chowning's Tavern were very dark in color; the first may be an African American, but the second looks more alien.

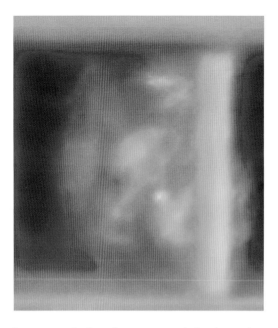 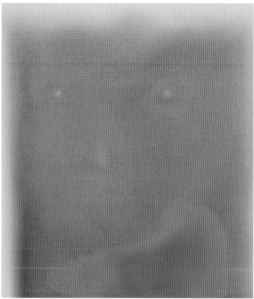

By contrast, the faces here were overly bright in color and perhaps equally as strange in their own way.

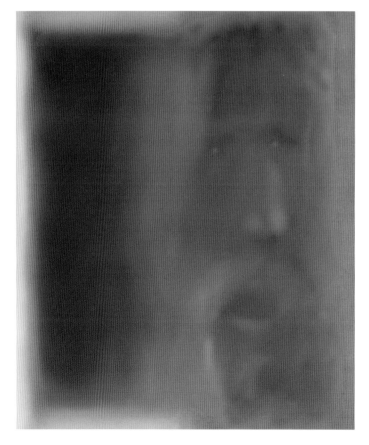

This fellow looks a bit too old to be the young Confederate soldier enamored with the waitress . . .

KING'S ARM TAVERN

The Mischievous Manager

This chapter reminds us that not all of the ghosts in Colonial Williamsburg are "colonial," or even nineteenth-century. The King's Arm Tavern, like all of Williamsburg's working taverns (Chowning's, Shield's, and Christiana Campbell's), is not an original building—it has, however, been rebuilt over the original foundation. But unlike nearby Shield's Tavern, whose ghost is very likely the murdered tavern owner from the eighteenth century (John Marot), the King's Arm Tavern has a ghost purportedly born in the twentieth century.

As an employee of nearby Shield's Tavern, word about the ghost of King's Arm Tavern got around to us—employees like to exchange ghost stories: *She* was the manager of the King's Arm Tavern (restaurant), and she happened to live in the apartment upstairs (before it was converted to more tavern space). If you recall, early on in the first book, I told you that the restored homes in Colonial Williamsburg are often rented out to employees, who must abide by a long list of rules to keep the area looking as it did in the eighteenth century. Exceptions are the very haunted front part of the Peyton Randolph House, as well as the St. George Tucker House—a place for the most generous donors to the Colonial Williamsburg Foundation to stay when they come to visit. So the manager of the King's Arm, whose name was Irma, conveniently had her residence overhead so that she was always available for a problem or crisis. One Saturday morning, Betty, the head hostess, came to work early as she always did on

Saturdays to go up to Irma's apartment where the two would read and discuss the newspaper over tea. She found that the always-reliable Irma was not up for work, and she had this incredible yet unexplainable feeling of dread, and because of it she refused to go upstairs to Irma's apartment to check on her. Rather than ascend the stairs she waited for the assistant manager to arrive; she quickly sent him upstairs to investigate. After repeated knocks, he bent down to look through the keyhole and could see the lifeless manager lying on the floor. Irma had died the night before, which was why the always-punctual manager had not shown up for work. According to the employee I spoke with, this all occurred in the early days of the King's Arms Tavern. Today the apartment is no longer there; Colonial Williamsburg changed it over to additional restaurant space—but apparently Irma is . . .

One of the stairways to the upstairs portion of the present-day restaurant is quite steep, and waiters and waitresses ascend them with serving trays that are heavy. Every once in a while one of them will lose their balance, and they are caught and held up—*by an unseen force*. The grateful employees keep this story alive, because evidently Irma is still on managerial duty. Yes, Irma still inspects the restrooms, because many tourists have seen her in the bathroom mirror—both in the men's and women's facilities. But when the witnesses turn around to see the woman behind them looking in the mirror, she is gone—or she only appears in the mirror.

Irma has a mischievous side too: Sometimes in the evening when an employee blows out all of the candles in one room and starts blowing them out in another, he or she will turn around to find all of the candles lit again in the room they'd started in. She also likes to move things; through the years there have been many occasions when she has taken all of the candles and hurricane globes (glass enclosure placed around the candle) in one room and placed them all on the floor. She is very careful, however—for none of the candles or their fragile glass enclosure are ever broken or damaged by the ghost. Some say this only happens when she doesn't like a manager or employee. She opened a window in her former apartment one night, and it caught the eye of the manager as he was leaving; when he went up to close it, he found that the window was closed and locked. This same manager, on another evening, felt the cold chill of Irma's ghost on his neck the whole time he walked through the tavern to close it up. At the front door and apparently afraid the ghost would follow him home, he exclaimed, "Irma, leave me alone!"—and the ghost immediately departed. Overall, Irma is a benevolent ghost who wants to take care of the restaurant that she was put in charge of—she thinks she still runs the place . . . do you?

There are a lot of geo-light apparitions overhead the tavern on moonlit nights, and a lot of faces in the windows. I cannot say with any certainty that one of the faces is Irma, but it is a possibility! One phantom that I found here reminded me of one I found at the powder magazine—do they belong to the same family? Look at the photos from the powder magazine, and compare that to the photos here at the King's Arms Tavern. Do you see a similarity between any of the faces?

Here is the King's Arm Tavern with several apparitions overhead.

Or could *this* gap-mouthed ghost be Irma, or is it someone else in the long history of this tavern?

Is this Irma, the former manager of the King's Arms Tavern? Or is it someone else who lived and died on this property? Some have suggested that this is an eighteenth-century man in a wig—but I have no idea if what is surrounding his face is hair or just the ephemeral mist that sometimes surrounds ghosts— what do you think?

Could this trio be customers from the heyday of
the King's Arms Tavern?

SHIELDS TAVERN

The Murdered Marot

A Personal Connection

I worked at Shields Tavern for a little more than a year while I went to the College of William and Mary. During that time, I heard hushed conversations about lights turning on without the aid of human hands, footsteps in the night at closing time not made by human feet, locking and unlocking doors (including the handicapped bathroom door), and about an eighteenth-century man in a tricorner hat. The phantom has been seen upstairs and strangely enough in a downstairs mirror. But when you look out into the tavern, this man is not there—only in the mirror! (Isn't that the opposite of what you've always heard in the movies and/or read in books—or is that only about vampires? You can see a vampire but he or she has no reflection in the mirror?) People on the street (both tourists and Colonial Williamsburg employees) have seen this man in the upstairs window looking down at them. Once you see the photographs it should be no surprise that this man usually hangs out upstairs—because a prominent spherical torch hangs over the very large chimney that sits in the middle of this very long tavern.

History of the Tavern and the Murdered Marot

James Shields, the original owner of this lot, sold it and the building on it to a French Huguenot (Protestant) named Jean (French for John) Marot in 1708. Marot's Ordinary was in business in 1705, so evidently Marot leased property somewhere in Williamsburg for three years before he bought the Shields' property. Marot had immigrated to Virginia in 1700, and would soon marry Ann Pasteur, with whom he had three daughters: Edith, Ann, and Rachel. Marot served as William Byrd's secretary—the mega-rich man who could never live within his means—for several years before applying for a license to operate an ordinary at the Shields' property. Marot operated the tavern from 1705 until 1717, when he was mortally wounded by fellow tavern keeper and supposed friend Francis Sharpe. Marot was forty years old at the time, and although Sharpe was put on trial for murder, he evidently was acquitted because records show him purchasing a license for a tavern several years later.

Many feel that the murdered Marot is the man haunting the reconstructed Shields Tavern—although the wine cellar is original. Later on, James Shields (II) married Jean's daughter, Ann Marot; they kept the tavern under the Shields name until Shields' death in 1750. Ann kept the tavern for two years after her husband died, and then, unfortunately, she met and married Henry Whetherburn—remember the man everyone in Williamsburg considered a murderous husband from the first book? (Go back to it for the full story of the Whetherburn family.) Ann's daughter mysteriously got pregnant and named the son she had after her "stepfather," Henry, who doted on the boy and willed his whole estate to him. Foul play? You be the judge. The tavern's wooden structure burned in 1858. It was sold as a vacant lot to Colonial Williamsburg, and the wooden structure you see today was built over the original wine cellar in 1989.

"Shields Tavern Is Loaded with Ghosts!"

According to many of the employees who work/have worked in Shields Tavern at night, they echo the sentiment of one waiter: "Shields Tavern is loaded with ghosts!" One of the most obvious explanations for the paranormal activity is the murdered Jean Marot, but there are a few other characters that may take part. First let's take a look at possible hauntings by the former owner.

Here is a story related by a former chef that worked at Shields: One late night at closing time, the manager did her walkthrough of the entire restaurant, checking that all lights and candles were out on all three floors, the doors were all locked, and that everything was in order for the next morning's shift. The original wine cellar is part of the restaurant, but attached to that is an underground kitchen and a tunnel underneath the gardens in the back to a shed on Francis Street were employees can enter and exit the restaurant without being seen. So after going through this whole process and exiting the shed, the manager looks back at the tavern one last time, and she sees that the lights are on! So she goes back to the shed, down the stairs, through the tunnel, through the kitchen, through the wine cellar, up the stairs to the main floor, and up the stairs to the second floor to turn the lights out—again. After turning out all the lights a second time she goes through the whole convoluted process of exiting the building. She exits the shed and looks back at Shields Tavern—and the lights are all back on! So back inside the shed she went, down the stairs, through the tunnel,

through the kitchen, through the wine cellar, up the stairs, through the main floor, up the stairs to the second floor, and this time *all the furniture was rearranged!* All the tables are in one room, all of the chairs are in another, and the manager is now at her wits end.

"Please! I just need to be done!" She cried out to the prankster poltergeist.

So she went through the whole process of turning out all the lights—but no, she was just too tired to put all the tables and chairs back. She went back through the whole process of exiting the tavern again, and turned around to look back at Shields; the lights were still off, and she was able to go home. She came in the next day for her managerial shift, and the first thing she did was go to the opening manager to apologize about the chairs and tables. But he was confused and said that nothing was out of place when he opened the tavern. So she had to explain what happened the previous evening for him to understand what she meant.

Many have seen a dark figure in the windows upstairs, and think that the phantom is Jean Marot; evidently Jean listened to the weary manager the third and final time she came in to turn out the lights, and was nice enough to put all the furniture back. I guess he understands how exhausted you can get when you manage a tavern . . .

Another frequently seen wraith at the tavern is a woman in an exquisite green dress, who some believe may have been the victim of a plague or influenza. She likes to appear in mirrors, and according to a tavern program supervisor, especially to new employees when they peer into the mirrors, to give them a fright that startles them to the reality that their workplace is haunted. Some of them think she is the one who plays with the lights and also rearranges the table settings.

A ghost tour guide for the "tavern ghost walks" was in the middle of her tour at Shields when several tourists had to use the restroom.

She opened the closed restaurant and took her tour in so that those who needed to could go to the restroom. She led her tour back outside the tavern, and asked them to wait a minute while she used the restroom herself. After she finished she went to the door to discover that she could not get out—even though the door only locks from the inside. After she struggled a while with the door, she could hear laughter right outside, and then she heard a click and was able to open the door. I don't know what it is about locking a woman in the restroom, but this story sounds eerily similar to the one at Chowning's.

Some tourists have seen phantom diners in the lower room of Shields; a couple insisted that the tavern had to be open because they saw a man and a woman dining by candlelight when they walked by—the only problem is the tavern was closed. The manager had just set the room up for the next day, so he knew that there were no diners in that room, and no candle had been lit in the room the whole day. So for the next few minutes the manager had to argue with this couple that the tavern was closed and that there were no diners eating there. So just how do you politely tell a customer that the diners that they see are not real—they are ghosts? Do you insult them by saying that they did not see what they insist they saw, or do you admit that your establishment has ghosts?

When I worked at Shields' Tavern during my college years, I met a man who worked for Colonial Williamsburg as an interpreter/actor, and he would periodically come into the tavern in eighteenth-century attire and portray James Shields. His name was John Lowe. When I met John he must have been in his late sixties or older, and he was a big man with an affable charm. He stayed in character while he spoke with the diners (as well as the waiters), going from table to table to discuss both how much they enjoyed his food and the latest in eighteenth-

century news. He could be a bit forgetful, and although he remembered our faces he could not remember the names of the wait staff. Despite his forgetfulness, I always enjoyed his portrayal of James Shields whenever he came to my station. I was not surprised to hear of John's passing from a woman who wrote to Colonial Williamsburg about him. She first spoke about her experiences as a diner when John would come, and how John, who would "kind of remember" them, would involve her in a conversation to loosen everybody else up and involve them in the interactive theater of Colonial Williamsburg.

This woman and her husband had lunch at Shields' during Christmas shortly after John died, and the woman went downstairs to the cellar to use the restroom. She noted that although it was a cold day, the heat was on throughout the building, and she was quite comfortable until she got to the bottom of the stairs. There she was confronted with a very cold breeze that swirled around her— even though the outside door was closed tight. Although she was not even thinking about John at the time, she insists that she felt John's presence. This happened a second time during another visit to the tavern, and she is certain that the former actor is now haunting Shield's, and that he now watches over the old tavern—I wonder what James Shields or Jean Marot thinks?

The following photos show the ghosts that I found at Shields; compare the facial expressions of each man. The facial expression of the first and third face indicates anger—don't you think? Is either one the murdered Marot? Or is he the darker face in the second photo? (Keep in mind that a dark face does not always indicate an African-American; facial features do.) It's ironic that the faces showed up in the downstairs window when so much of the paranormal activity is upstairs; but then again ghosts are attracted to light.

Here you can see Shield's Tavern with a prominent spherical apparition over the large central chimney.

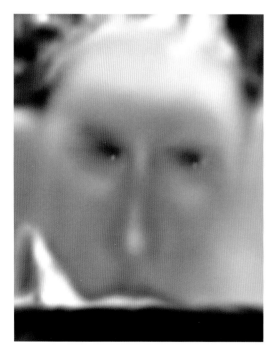

Could one of these be the rather angry face of the murdered Marot? Both appeared in the same window (different panes).

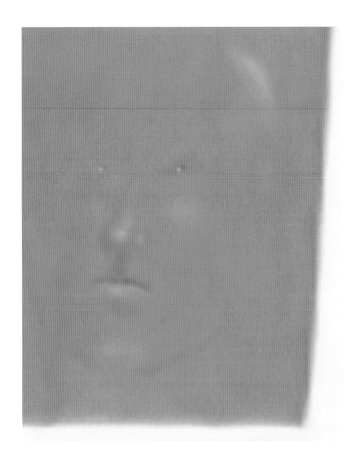

These two men appeared at the back of the building in the same window; the first man has a furrowed brow as if he is really angry—perhaps over being murdered?

THE BRICKHOUSE TAVERN

The "Stink of a Man"

History

One of only a few brick structures in the city of Williamsburg, the Brickhouse Tavern was a landmark in the eighteenth century, and today is known for the haunted lodging provided by Colonial Williamsburg. This building offers a little more than the typical haunted fare of disembodied footsteps and the "feeling" of being watched—the ghosts actually are willing to climb into bed with you—but wait, I'm getting ahead of the history:

This eighty-foot brick structure with complete cellars (unusual for Williamsburg's high water table) was more akin to an eighteenth-century strip mall, with various shops and businesses renting a portion of the building: a wig-maker, surgeon and apothecary, blacksmith, millinery, as well as its use as a tavern. This long brick house was built before 1761, and with four entrances was divided up between various tenants—even the cellar was divided and separately rented. In 1760, when the building was sold, Christiana Campbell leased it as a tavern when the transaction was made. She will show up in the next chapter with her own tavern, both which were frequented by George Washington, as he was a member of her exclusive club—more on that later.

After the Diggs family of Yorktown, a succession of Williams owned the building. William Withers sold the building to William Holt, a merchant in 1760, who would later sell it to William Carter, a surgeon and an apothecary in 1761, all in the colonial capital of Williamsburg. Is that enough of William for one sentence? Carter would hold on to the building from then till the end of the eighteenth century, but its heyday would be as a tavern first under Campbell, and then under Mary Davis from 1770 to 1773, when it was known as the Brickhouse Tavern. What's unusual about the tavern under Mary Davis was that it had rooms available for men *and women*, according to her ad in the local newspaper, the *Virginia Gazette*, on March 29, 1770 (she speaks about herself in the third person):

The subscriber [Mary Davis] begs leave to inform the Public in general, and her friends in particular, that she has removed from Lester's ferry, and rented Dr. Carter's large brick house, on the Main Street in Williamsburg; where she proposes to accommodate Ladies and Gentlemen with private lodgings. She has 12 or 14 very good lodging rooms with fire places in most of them, which will hold two or three beds in each; she is willing to rent out some of them yearly to such as may incline to find their own beds and furniture. The rooms above are convenient for Gentlemen, those below for Ladies; the house consisting of two parts, and divided lengthwise by a brick partition . . .

Women did not do a lot of traveling in the eighteenth century, and if they did, they would usually stay at the home of family or friends, and this ad is a first for the taverns of

Williamsburg. Taverns, for the most part, were meant to accommodate men of the upper and middling classes. American women had started to question their subservient role in a male-dominated society, so Mary Davis, perhaps in an effort to get more women to travel, both advertised and made provisions for the women to stay in the downstairs rooms in the tavern, and the men would sleep in the upstairs rooms. But notice she also offers private lodgings, which came with a price. Otherwise the eighteenth-century norm was to have multiple beds in a room, with multiple people to a bed. Men in the eighteenth century thought nothing of crawling into a bed with several other men; keep that thought in mind when we begin the discussion on ghosts . . .

A raging fire took down the Brickhouse Tavern in April of 1842—a fire so intense that it took out the whole block of homes facing the Duke of Gloucester Street. All that was left of the tavern was the brick shell and cellar, which filled with water and became the playground for young boys in Williamsburg. During the summer months, according to a Williamsburg resident, they sailed homemade ships over the tiny, man-made pond; during the winter months it was their ice-skating rink. Ten years later, after the Battle of Williamsburg (also called the Battle of Fort Magruder—May 5, 1862) the Union set up camp in Williamsburg and blasted the former tavern in order to use the bricks for their fortifications. Whatever was left was pulled down in 1870, to build a large frame house, ending the saga of the Brickhouse Tavern till its reconstruction by Colonial Williamsburg.

Today, the Brickhouse Tavern once again opens its doors to travelers, however they are not required to share a bed with anyone. Perhaps this memo was not given to the eighteenth-century travelers that still reside there . . .

The "Stink of a Man"

First off, we have some of the standard haunting fare, including heavy footsteps, invisible keys jangling, shadow people, lights and faucets being turned on and off, and the sweet smell of tobacco (different from the tobacco products that are smoked today), even though smoking is forbidden in the building. But wait—that's just the innocuous stuff: Some of the guests have experienced sleep paralysis—being awakened and yet unable to move. Some have the covers taken off during the night and wake up freezing—with perhaps the ghostly presence contributing to the icy feeling. Guests have experienced visible figures walking through their rooms, and sometimes exiting out a window or through a solid wall.

But the most popular story (at least that anyone will own up to) is that of two sisters who made an annual visit to the tavern. Have you ever been awakened by the scent of something? One sister woke up from a sound sleep to the combined smell of sweet tobacco and the "stink of a man" (her words, not mine)—the sweaty stench of a man who had not bathed in a long time. She opened her eyes to find a man sitting on her bed, with greasy long hair and his sleeves rolled up to his elbows. She felt sorry for him . . . until he placed one hand on the wall and then he appeared to lean in towards her as if he was going to plant a kiss on her face. Shocked, she sat up screaming, and the brazen ghost promptly disappeared. The other sister woke up from the scream, and they both decided that they felt safer with lights and the television on for the remainder of the night. If you decide to stay at the Brickhouse Tavern, and you catch the same scent—the "stink of a man,"—you may want to keep your eyes closed . . . or else pucker up!

Here is a partial photo of the eighty-foot-long Brickhouse Tavern with the full moon's edge appearing over the peak of the roof. (The tree blocks a full view at either angle.)

The Brickhouse Tavern was unusual in the fact that it allowed women to stay in the downstairs rooms. Perhaps this is the face of an eighteenth-century woman traveler—or the face of Mary Davis, the woman who ran the tavern.

Another strange photo of what appears to be a young man; could that be a streak of light from another ghost by his ear, or does it look pointed to you?

A photo of a boy or young man, with an eye for an ear . . .

Could this be the ghost of the man with the long greasy hair who sat on the edge of a guest's bed and then tried to give her a kiss?

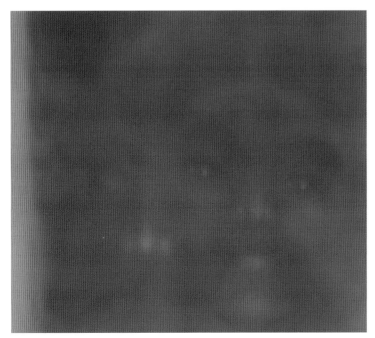

These two (especially the man on the right) look to be nineteenth-century occupants, during or after the Civil War.

More female occupants of the tavern or travelers from the late eighteenth century? Perhaps one of these two is Mary Davis?

CHRISTIANA CAMPBELL'S TAVERN

By George—the Gathering, the Gambling,
and the Ghosts

One of the finest taverns in all of Williamsburg hosted the likes of George Washington, Thomas Jefferson, and many of the other members of the House of Burgesses when it was in session. Washington was particularly fond of the seafood served at Christiana Campbell's Tavern, and he even wrote in his journal that he dined there ten times in two months. Washington would often record his frequent visits to "Mrs. Campbell's" during the 1760s and 1770s, when he attended the General Assembly. He also mentioned when he would dine in *the Club*, a private room reserved for regular customers—modeled after the fashionable London coffee houses. Washington was a Mason, and the Williamsburg Masonic Lodge regularly held social events at this tavern.

Governor Fauquier, a man with his own personal cook, not only dined here but also documented an historical event happening right outside the tavern from his seat on the porch—a menacing crowd protesting the Stamp Act in 1765. (May I also state that another document states that this event took place at the Charlton Coffee House.) They were there undoubtedly to make sure the crown's representative in Virginia witnessed their dissatisfaction with taxation without representation.

I'm sure you've heard the old realtor adage touting the three most important selling points of real estate: *Location, location, location*. It seemed that Christiana Campbell's had it, because not only was her tavern just a short walk from the back of the Capitol building, but it overlooked Waller Street—essentially the stock market for the Colony of Virginia.

No, it was not a specific building, but an *open street* where money exchanged hands for business and trade. (In case you didn't notice the similarities: Virginia had Waller Street, and New York has Wall Street.) Like other *publick houses* in Virginia, Campbell's tavern also served as an eighteenth-century casino. Prominent politicians, businessmen, and planters (often in the same person) were quite the gamblers, such as Williams Byrd III (who despite his massive land and business holdings was always in debt, and ended up committing suicide), and the tavern tables would often be battered from their gaming boxes. So perhaps some of the ghosts are gamblers who may have lost their fortunes over the gaming tables in this tavern.

The building is a former residence, built in 1754, by printer and deputy postmaster John Stretch. The building was also used as a playhouse before it was converted to a tavern by Jane Vobe, the woman who would later move her business to run a tavern (the King's Arms Tavern) on the other side of the Capitol. Now that you know about the tavern building, let's take a look at the woman who ran one of Williamsburg's most successful taverns for more than thirty years.

Christiana Burdett (her maiden name) Campbell was the daughter of a Williamsburg innkeeper who began operating an ordinary, (public house, tavern, bed and breakfast, and restaurant are words that all apply) upon her return to Williamsburg around the year 1755. She was born circa 1723, and left shortly after her father's death in 1746, to marry Ebenezer

Campbell, an apothecary (pharmacist for dispensing natural cures) who lived in the town of Blandford, a town near Petersburg—south of Richmond. It was a marriage that was short-lived—Ebenezer died fewer than six years later. The couple did have two children, Mary (nicknamed Molly) in about 1750, and Ebenezer (nicknamed Ebe) was born sometime after the father's death in 1752. Yes, she named the poor girl Ebenezer after her deceased father; hopefully her friends only knew her as Ebe. After the birth of Ebe and the estate sale, Christiana returned to Williamsburg in October of 1753, with her two girls and began a new phase of her life about 1760.

With Ebe about eight years old and Molly about ten, both girls would have been old enough to help their mother start a tavern. The funds from the death of her husband were probably running out, and the single mother probably felt the need to generate income. As far as her options, it made sense that she would go into the tavern business—something she'd experienced as a child, so she was probably familiar with all the essential duties of a tavern-keeper.

She began her business renting the James Anderson House, had a stint at the Brickhouse Tavern (the Brickhouse Tavern Historical Report states this, but it is left out of Colonial Williamsburg's Historical Bio of Campbell), and later (but briefly) the R. Charlton Coffeehouse, before first renting and then later buying a tavern that bore her name in 1771. She enjoyed a great deal of success until Governor Thomas Jefferson moved the state capital to Richmond in 1780, subsequently followed by an economic decline that would transform Williamsburg from the bustling capital of Virginia to a sleepy farming town. I've come across conflicting records, some saying she closed the doors by 1783, and others

Here's George Washington's favorite place to dine in Williamsburg: Christiana Campbell's Tavern.

saying 1787. A young businessman from Yorktown, Andrew Macaulay, who evidently had experienced Campbell's Tavern in its heyday, was shocked when he returned in February of 1783, to find that the pug-nosed "landlady, a little old woman about four feet high and equally thick" no longer operated the tavern. Evidently, someone else was operating the tavern when they returned, who led the man and his wife into the parlor, and Macaulay wrote that "the house had a cold, poverty struck appearance," and they quickly left.

Two records say that Christiana moved to Fredericksburg to live out her last few years with her married daughter, Ebe, and her family. She died about ten years after the tavern closed, in March of 1792. The tavern stood on the market for about ten years after Christiana died before anyone purchased it; if it looked poverty struck in 1783, can you imagine what it looked like after about two decades with no tenants or owners? The neglected tavern burned down in 1859, and the vacant lot would wait almost one hundred years before the tavern would be rebuilt (beginning in 1954) and reopened to its now historical status as the place where Washington and Jefferson dined. I think the many ghosts that reside here have waited patiently for the return of the popular tavern—now they are free to watch you dine—and who knows, perhaps Washington and/or Jefferson stop by every once in a while to reminisce about *the Club*! (Lincoln is said to haunt four different places; perhaps these larger-than-life men do likewise!)

When I photographed Christiana Campbell's Tavern, I had several people with me; they immediately noticed that a light seemed to be going on, then off again, in the top right dormer window of the *closed* tavern. Were they trying to get our attention? I was able to capture a clear face in the window where the light was being turned on and off, as well as a lot more faces in the windows of the first floor. Not all of the faces were clear enough to put in this chapter, but let me assure you that a plethora of ghosts reside here; care to dine with them?

A downstairs apparition; the hairstyle appears to be twentieth century—perhaps a waiter from the tavern's recent past?

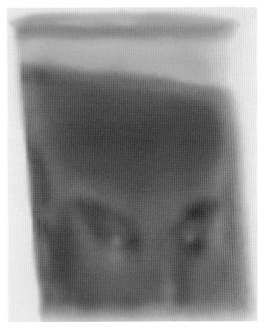

Another ghost with alien eyes . . .

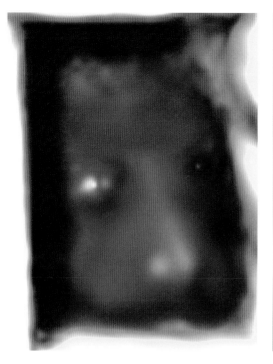

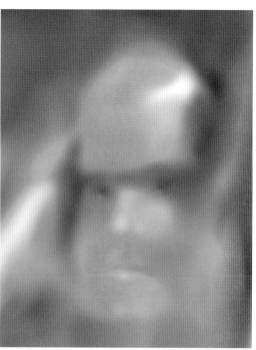

Perhaps an African American with the intimidating light-eye/dark-eye characteristic that continues to beg the question: "What does it mean?"

This bald man appeared in a downstairs window near the front door.

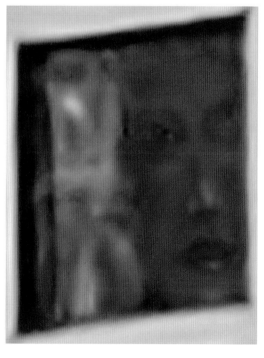

An African American—perhaps a slave during the apex of the tavern's popularity?

A feminine face in the next window looks like she's wearing lipstick.

This was the clearest of all the faces, and he almost
looks like Washington. But then again they say he
haunts Mt. Vernon—could he be in two places in the
afterlife? Check out the column of white apparitions
next to the faces of this photo and the next two.

STACKING APPARITIONS AND THE ARMISTEAD HOUSE

The Original Totem

History

Seeing new phenomena can be both a blessing and a curse. If you look at the last three faces from the previous chapter, you may see what I'm alluding to. Discovering something for the first time is the blessing, wrapping your head around what it all means can be the curse. When I say discovering for the first time, I'm talking about a personal discovery for myself. I'm saying that because I believe Native Americans of the Northwest (of North America) have already experienced what I'm about to show you, and I believe they have memorialized their discovery in a specific artistic endeavor. Part of the Northwestern Native American culture is to take the trunk of the cedar tree (chosen for its ability to resist rot and insects), which is plentiful there, and carve it into a series of faces or effigies, one stacked right on top of another: A totem pole. (Might I also add that the Algonquian Indians, particularly the members of the Powhatan Confederacy in eastern Virginia, carved totem poles for dance ceremonies? Unlike the Northwestern tribes, these totems traditionally have a carved face at the top only, sometimes accompanied by pictographs below the carving.) Although this is not about their religious dogma—it is more for aesthetic value—it nevertheless can be tied to their belief in an afterlife. Among the faces you will see carved into the totem pole will be family members (to be honored),

animals (chosen to be a part of the family's crest), and *depictions of the supernatural.* Totems can be anywhere from three to more than twenty meters tall, created to document a family's power, history, crest animal(s), and their personal experiences with the supernatural. Some totems, by contrast, have been made to bring shame and embarrassment on another family; for example shaming a tribe, group, or family who has not paid their debts, or even a totem protesting the decisions or conduct of the government.

Although Northwest totems come in a variety of sizes, colors, shapes, and meanings, they all have one thing in common: They are comprised of a series of faces (whether animal or human)—one stacked right on top of another. I believe the totem pole began as an artistic depiction of a paranormal experience; someone was able to see what I call *stacking apparitions.* I have said before that it sometimes appears to be a competition to be seen: Multiple faces appearing in windows, some of them complete, some just a partial face, in some cases just eyes. But this new phenomena has faces, usually the unrecognizable classic whites, stacking on top of each other. I can only think that this is some kind of symbiotic relationship, where they are pooling their energy to make themselves *collectively* visible to the camera's and sometimes the human's eye.

Christiana Cambel's Tavern was a good segue into this chapter, because if you look back, you can see several examples of stacking apparitions. Compare those to ones seen at the Armistead House.

The Armistead House

The second and third examples of stacking apparitions are from the Armistead House, a home built in the Victorian era, circa 1890, but not the Bowden Armistead House that you saw in the first book. Once a family of opulent wealth, that all changed when the Union confiscated the Armistead Estate after the Civil War. Cary Peyton Armistead could no longer live off of his family's financial assets and had to go to work as a lawyer. In addition to his law practice, he became a steward for the Eastern State Hospital and a director for the Peninsula Bank. Although he never restored his family to the wealth and prestige of the antebellum years, he did have this house built on the site of the Charlton Coffee House. He lived here with his wife and five children till his death in 1901, in his early forties. His wife would outlive him by forty years, and when she died, the house became a bed and breakfast, renting out rooms for tourists from the 1940s, until the death of the last child, Dora Armistead in 1984. As for the other children, one son died very young in 1909, two other children died in the 1940s, not too long after their mother died, and the first of the two longest-living sisters (Cara) died in the late 1970s.

Like their mother Endora, Cara and Dora Armistead were against selling the family home to Colonial Williamsburg—even if they were allowed to live the remainder of their lives in the home without charge. They could not afford to keep the house without some form of income, so the remaining two siblings rented rooms to tourists until their deaths, Cara in 1979, and Dora in 1984. Cara was

more of an extrovert and enjoyed playing host to guests in her home; Dora, the introvert, put up with the inconvenience only to keep the family home from being sold to Colonial Williamsburg. After Dora's death the house was leased and operated as a museum from 1985 until 1993, by the Association for the Preservation of Virginia Antiquities, when it was no longer deemed profitable. The family's lifelong effort to keep their house and property out of the hands of the Colonial Williamsburg Foundation came to an end in 1995: The house's owners, retired Circuit Court Judge Robert Armistead, his wife, and his sister (owners of the Bowden Armistead House next to Bruton Parish Church) leased the property to Colonial Williamsburg for seventy-five years with the stipulation that the Armistead house would be moved to another nearby lot that was not part of the historic area. So, presently, the house has been moved to its new location, and Robert T. Armistead is the final holdout to Colonial Williamsburg.

I thought it strange that out of a family of five children, none of the Armistead children left the home they were born in during their lifetime, either in pursuit of a career or to get married and raise a family of their own. Dora Armistead, the last sibling to live in the house, neither liked her role as a host to tourists in the family homestead, nor the thought of selling out to Colonial Williamsburg, which makes her post-mortem occupation of the house even more interesting.

Even though the house has been moved, Dora has found her way to its new location, and is said to be unhappy about the move and when the curious stand and stare at her home from the street. A large group of tourists witnessed the curtains in the upstairs bedroom (Dora's) blowing violently when the home was unoccupied and all of the doors and windows were locked. Others have gotten the feeling that someone was staring at them from the house. When I saw the home, there were no curtains in the windows to move around, and since I have no psychic abilities, I felt nothing when I photographed the place. But you will see that the house is occupied—from the looks of things not only by Dora but perhaps the whole family! I have no way of knowing for sure, but from the multiple stacking apparitions, the house is busy with activity from the afterlife! Now that you know the background, and how the parents and all five children lived out their lives in this very house, it's no wonder that I've captured a stacking apparition here—they are all still together in the afterlife! Notice that first set of stacking apparitions at the Armistead House looks like little chrome skulls; the second set is in a more agreeable color to the sisters. The question is—are they both made up of the same ghosts?

So I have become privy to something that Northwestern Native Americans have known for years: Multiple ghost heads will sometimes stack on top of each other in windows in a symbiotic ensemble that Native Americans have memorialized in totem poles. I wonder if this type of cooperation only occurs with families (like the Armisteads) or if it's more of a matter of proximity. I know this—I will never look at a totem pole the same way again; will you?

This is the second Armstead House in Williamsburg, formerly on the Duke of Gloucester Street right by the Capitol, with huge apparitions around it. When the last Armstead sister passed on, the property was leased to Colonial Williamsburg, and the building was moved out of the restored area. Perhaps all the Armstead siblings haunt this home, even though it was moved.

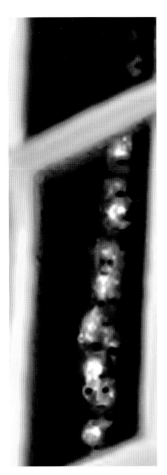

Here are two examples of stacking apparitions, both at the Armstead House. One looks like little chrome skulls, and the other is accompanied by two faces.

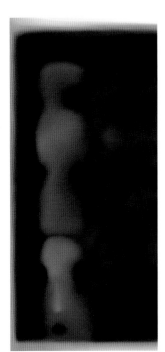

A stacking apparition from the Thomas Nelson Jr. house.

THE CAPITOL

*The Haunted Portrait of Patrick Henry and the
Headless Statesman*

History

Virginia's General Assembly is the oldest elected representative body in the United States in continuous operation, starting in 1619, as the House of Burgesses in Jamestown, moving to Williamsburg in 1699, and then it became the legislative body of the independent state of Virginia in 1776. Fire burned the "Virginia Statehouse" at Jamestown in 1698, for the third time, and that's when legislators decided to move the seat of government inland to a place known as Middle Plantation, which was quickly renamed Williamsburg in honor of the current reigning monarch. The first American structure to which the word "Capitol" would be applied was completed in 1705, although anxious legislators, tired of meeting in William and Mary's Wren Building, had their first session in the incomplete building in April of 1704. The original building was devoid of fireplaces and chimneys in order to prevent what happened at Jamestown three times, and candles and pipes were also banned. In 1723, the secretary complained that the building was too damp, and so chimneys and fireplaces were added. (Do you see where this is going?) The Capitol burned in 1747. Governor Gooch urged that a new building be built, and by a narrow two-vote margin, a new building was approved; some legislators wanted the Capitol moved to a place more accessible to trade and navigation. The new building had squared edges on the southern façade; the Capitol

building rebuilt by Colonial Williamsburg is true to the original building built in 1705, with an architectural feature that is both more beautiful, more expensive, and more difficult to build: rounded corners.

Quite a few events took place in this new Capitol that were precursors to independence; the first was a defiant and passionate speech against the crown on May 29, 1765.Patrick Henry delivered his famous "Caesar-Brutus" speech against the Stamp Act. For some of the more conservative legislators it was over the top, but they would eventually come around to Henry's way of thinking. For those who gathered on May 15, 1776, there was a unanimous vote for independence, making Virginia the first state to do so. When Thomas Jefferson moved the Capitol to Richmond in 1780, to get it out of range of British naval artillery, and conveniently closer to his home I might add (Jefferson's less-than-affectionate term for Williamsburg was "Devilsburg"), the building where history was made, where suppers, dances, and social events were held, became a vacant shell. The once proud Capitol building of the first and largest colony in North America served as an admiralty court, a law school, a military hospital, a grammar school, and a female academy, suffered an undeserving and ignominious ending: The west wing was sold for its bricks and demolished just four years later (1793); the east side burned in 1832, ending the legacy of Virginia's most historic government building. What were they thinking?

Ghosts in a Reconstructed Building?

In 1934, the reconstructed Capitol was dedicated with a lot of fanfare, and on opening day of that year, President Franklyn D. Roosevelt had the presidential motorcade drive up Duke of Gloucester Street pronouncing the street that runs from the Wren Building to the newly rebuilt Capitol "the most historical avenue in all America." Evidently, the ghosts approved—because they took up residence there—as you will soon see by the photographs.

One popular ghost story that has been passed around for years is that Patrick Henry, George Washington, George Mason, Thomas Jefferson, and the ghosts of other Virginia legislators gather at midnight on July 4th to commemorate independence. I know of one of Colonial Williamsburg's security guards who worked at night who went there several years in a row to see if he could witness this historic rendezvous—he left disappointed each time. On a more realistic note, interpreters and tourists alike have heard the sounds of legislative debates (or is it court cases being argued?) coming from the dark, empty halls of the Capitol, in a way similar to the paranormal activity heard at the Raleigh Tavern—sounds of activity emanating from a darkened building.

There are, however, more stories about Patrick Henry that are worth mentioning. The first story is along the same lines as the story above: The apparition of Patrick Henry is seen outside the Capitol every year at midnight on July 4th smiling, because his dream of liberty from the tyranny of England came true.

Another ghost story pertains to the portrait of Patrick Henry that hung in the Capitol. For years Colonial Williamsburg had a special portrait of the famous orator/statesman hanging there. But every year, the face of this self-taught lawyer would undergo a change that was witnessed by Colonial Williamsburg's interpreters and tourists, with no plausible explanation. For most of the year the portrait of Henry had a smiling face, but every spring, the face would turn from a smile to a noticeable frown—right up until the date of his famous "Caesar-Brutus" speech against the Stamp Act on May 29. Then the smile would return to Henry's face.

I met a Colonial Williamsburg interpreter who worked at the Capitol while the portrait was still up, and he said that he would get tired of telling curious tourists that he had no idea why the expression on Patrick Henry's face would change from a smile to a frown and back—although he really did, but remember, Colonial Williamsburg is all about the history—and not about ghosts. This anomaly was well known, because people would come from all over the country to see for themselves; some would even come in the spring and then later on in the summer to witness the change. Someone in management heard about the painting's changing expression, and subsequently Colonial Williamsburg took the painting out of the Capitol and put it into storage to return the public's attentions back towards the history. I wonder if Patrick Henry's painting has a frown all of the time now . . .

For the longest time, a few red super cells and a few white pillars were all I could capture at the rebuilt capital, but then one day I found the ghosts out and about. Perhaps the strangest of these was the headless man in eighteenth-century attire who appeared in one photo on the right side of the Capitol's walkway (along with a very wispy classic white) only to be found a few seconds later on the left side, and appeared to be conversing with a female phantom (who apparently was able to make her head appear) in a rather close proximity, too close for those of us who are living. A few gap-mouthed faces round out the phantom presence at the Capitol, including a fellow in a slanted hat and a man in a white shirt and tie—could this man have taken residence after the restoration in 1934, perhaps a former employee of Colonial Williamsburg? Whole-body apparitions like the eighteenth-century woman are pretty rare—but even the headless apparitions were an exhilarating find considering the norm for the capital.

Inevitably, this takes me back to my original assertion from the first book: You cannot spend one evening at a haunted site, like some of the paranormal shows on television, and expect to get good results. I guess the ghosts have to get to know you before they are willing to reveal themselves . . .

This is the Capitol on the night of the full moon, and to the right of the cupola is a large apparition.

This is my favorite Capitol capture: An almost invisible eighteenth-century man (probably a burgess considering how he is dressed) with glowing white eyes is confronted by a wispy classic white that is not-so-appropriately dressed. Is it a founding father? Perhaps Patrick Henry?

Here is a much more evanescent form of what I believe to be the same woman (in the previous photo) walking out in front of the Capitol.

Notice that the woman's face is plainly visible, but the man that she is facing has no face; there is almost nothing above that fancy collar that he's wearing! Is it the same man that's in the first photo?

This looks like a nineteenth-century man—perhaps a Civil War soldier—but what's he doing in the Capitol building, which no longer existed during the War Between the States? Did he die on the grounds of the building?

In the same building we have what appears to be a twentieth-century man dressed in a white shirt and tie, perhaps a former employee of Colonial Williamsburg? Does the Capitol have ghosts from three different centuries? The photos seem to be saying yes . . .

BLUE BELL

Politicians Cavorting with Women?

The Blue Bell Tavern was hidden on the other side of the capitol for good reason: It had a reputation to conceal. Yet it was right next to the Capitol—because the tavern's customers had a reputation to protect. But this part of the building's history is not brought up too often because Colonial Williamsburg wants to take the high road and emphasize history—mainly the road to independence. Rightly so, because a lot of children tour Williamsburg to learn firsthand of all the events leading up to the colony's call to separate from the control of Great Britain—and not the indiscretions of some of the politicians and founding fathers. Do you get where I'm going with this veiled, one-sided conversation? Let me put it to you this way: Williamsburg served as the capitol for the largest British colony in North America, and elected officials came from all over the "Old Dominion" to take part in the legislative activities of the House of Burgesses or the Governor's Council. The Blue Bell was the alleged home to the world's oldest profession, spoken of only in undertones and whispers; and politicians who were many miles away from their homes and families sometimes sought the companionship of women at the Blue Bell.

Although Williamsburg's court records were all lost during the Civil War, a Rachel Rodeway and Joan Clarke went on trial in York County for running a "disorderly house," eighteenth-century legal language for a brothel. The case was dismissed because it was being prosecuted in Williamsburg—but we have no idea what the particulars or the outcome was. Earlier, in 1713, Susanna Allen was accused not only of keeping a disorderly house, but also keeping company with a married man. The brothel charge was dismissed, but Ms. Allen did have to pay 500 pounds of tobacco to the Bruton Parish Church for keeping company with the married man—who evidently got off without so much as a slap on the wrist. Allen may not have gotten away with adultery, but the same court kept granting her a license to operate a tavern . . . Writer Harold Gill Jr. provided the details for the miscreancy of the women mentioned above; he doesn't seem to think that Williamsburg, a small rural town, could have supported a disorderly house.[1] David Doody is quoted in the same article on Colonial Williamsburg's website as saying historical evidence does not support the claim that the Blue Bell was a "bawdy house." But then again, in this town where the Bruton Parish Church watched the morals of the Williamsburg's residents, who's going to write about the existence of a brothel? Who's going to risk being fined and a marred reputation to investigate the goings on of a possible bawdy house? Taverns and theaters were known for their links to prostitution in the eighteenth century, but specific records about prostitution are not in Williamsburg's surviving records. So we have to go with the rumors, the whispers, and the legends if we want to believe what many residents and interpreters have thought for years—that the Blue Bell was the bawdy house, the disorderly house, the brothel, or whatever you would like to call it, for the eighteenth-century capitol of Virginia. The Blue Bell is where straying husbands, whether they were politicians away from home or itinerant businessmen, could find the company of a woman for a price.

According to the *Colonial Williamsburg Guidebook*, the Blue Bell was the location of a tavern, store, lodging house, gunsmith, and a rental property. The London owner of the property was informed of the bad reputation of the tenants he had in the building, described as "always nasty," and that their payment record was deplorable. So you can choose to believe the written record or the whispered record; what is said in the official guidebook or whispered as you pass by. What do you think—was it just "nasty" tenants, or was it the world's oldest profession? Perhaps you can ask the curious ghosts waiting at the window: Are they looking for potential clients—or just watching you walk by?

The Blue Bell Tavern, hidden on the backside of the Capitol, had something to hide and its customers had something to protect: their reputation.

Here are some of the past employees of the Blue Bell anxiously waiting for customers even though they are now unfit, or should we say unable, to conduct business. Doesn't the face on the left look like it's crying?

On one busy evening in December called Grand Illumination, Colonial Williamsburg lights a candle in every window, along with fireworks and placing natural, traditional decorations at the doors and windows of its houses. I captured a ghost following a tourist inside the Blue Bell just as the door was about to close. Care to go inside?

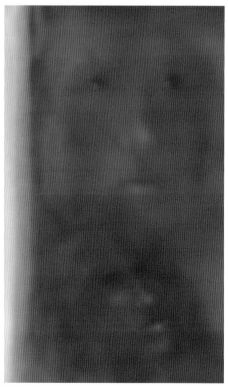

On a later outing, I captured these two faces in the same windowpane.

You have to look at this carefully, because another smaller face appears over the lower part of the larger face, creating an interesting anomaly.

CATHERINE BLAIKLEY HOUSE

The Famous Midwife: Does She Preside Over
Birth into the Afterlife?

History

On October 24, 1771, the *Virginia Gazette* ran this obituary:

[Deaths] Mrs. CATHERINE BLAIKLEY, of this City, in the seventy sixth Year of her Age; an eminent Midwife, and who, in the course of her Practice, brought upwards of three thousand Children into the World.

How many doctors can say that they delivered more than 3,000 children during the duration of their practice? You can see Catherine's tomb in the Bruton Parish Churchyard near the bell tower—the *Gazette* says that she died in her seventy-sixth year, but her tombstone says her seventy-third. Her husband was merchant William Blaikley, who died in 1736, leaving Catherine a widow for thirty-five years. William Blaikley was the owner of this lot by 1734, but only lived another two years, bequeathing it to Catherine. Williamsburg widows were frequently able to support themselves after their husbands died by making their homes into lodging houses, but Catherine Blaikley supported herself by delivering babies. The home was finally put up for auction in January 1773, and sold to Severinus Durfey, a tailor, and the Durfey family held on to the property till 1821. Colonial Williamsburg chose to name the home for this important woman who was instrumental in bringing more than 3,000 children into the world—in both Williamsburg and the surrounding counties, most likely both white and black—rather than Durfey. Even though Catherine did not survive the Revolutionary War years, her mark was indelible on the city.

The Blaikley home is not an original, and I did not expect to capture anything over it, but it was a beautiful moonlit night—the October full moon—so why not? To my surprise, I captured a bright spherical torch dominating the roof of this reconstructed house, and I was more surprised to find what I captured in the windows. I found a character that reminds me of a cartoon. This one filled up four windowpanes—most apparitions are only large enough to fill one, or even just a half of a pane. A second apparition looks like an older man with a beard lying down—perhaps on his deathbed? He has the look of fear in his eyes—what's he afraid of? Finally, I was able to capture the face of a young woman; is this face of a woman who died in childbirth? In the eighteenth century, a breech birth ended with the loss of both the mother and child—is that what happened here?

This is the Catherine Blaikley House, a reconstructed home that nevertheless has a few paranormal occupants, which include the bright spherical torch you see on the roof and several apparitions whose faces showed up in the windows.

This face occupies four windowpanes, which is highly unusual—the norm is just one.

This apparition appears to be lying down, with a genuine look of fear in his eyes as he tries to get up. The beard suggests a nineteenth-century gentleman around the period of the Civil War.

This photo looks like a young woman who may have died in her prime. Could she be a victim of a difficult childbirth? Notice that she has one normal colored eye and one dark eye . . .

PALMER HOUSE

Is the Slain Lieutenant Still in the House?

History

According to *Colonial Williamsburg: The Official Guide*, John Palmer built this original house on the site of an old store owned by jeweler Alexander Kerr. Palmer had a dual occupation: He was a lawyer as well as the bursar for the College of William and Mary. The previous house, "a well-finished brick house, in good repair," burned in April 1754, and a description of it burning appeared in the *William and Mary Quarterly*. The townspeople were afraid to get too near the place because there were two barrels of gunpowder stored there. An intrepid slave went inside the burning building and was able to remove one barrel, but the flames prevented him from returning. The powder ignited, and not only was the store consumed in flames, but the resulting explosion decimated the house's brick façade. Palmer rebuilt his home using a lot of the same bricks from the first house. (I wonder if he stored gunpowder in the new place?) In the eighteenth century, when masons bricked a building, they built a scaffold along the face of the structure that would leave spaces in the brick where the wood that supported the scaffolding was appropriately called *putlog holes*. When brickwork was finished, they would remove the scaffolding and fill the holes in with bricks and mortar. Palmer, however, liked the look of the holes in the brick and told the masons to leave them for a decorative effect, which you still see today (Sometime in the 1950s, one of the tenants placed apples in the holes at Christmas—a tradition that continues today). The Palmer House remained in the Palmer estate as a rental property for twenty years, until his daughters finally sold the home in 1780.

The house passed through many hands till a wealthy Williamsburg businessman purchased it in 1834. William W. Vest would later double the size of the original eighteenth-century house as well as add a large porch (all of which has been removed and the building restored to its eighteenth-century appearance). When the Peninsula Campaign of the Civil War began, Vest, as well as many other townspeople, left for the safety of Richmond. During his absence, Confederate General Magruder, as well as his replacement, used the house as their base of operations. After the Confederate retreat, Union General McClellan took over after Johnston evacuated the house; then Colonel Campbell, provost marshal for the Union forces, occupied the Palmer House on September 9, 1862. Campbell was taken as a Confederate prisoner-of-war when a Confederate cavalry raid caught the Union forces off-guard. David Cronin, a captain of the First New York Mounted Rifles would later take charge.

Cronin wrote of his experience enforcing marshal law in Williamsburg, noting that the residents despised the Union forces, looking at them with hatred and contempt. He also wrote that Williamsburg, the last Union outpost before the Confederate capital of Richmond, was ground zero for espionage. Clandestine observation from both sides of the war effort endeavored to learn what the other was planning, their troop numbers and movements, and their military arsenal and secrets. Cronin would later learn that the three slaves who took care of him at the Palmer House had delivered Union military secrets to the Confederates. On the other side of the coin, there were slaves who spied on Confederate forces.

In addition to slaves that spied for either side, some men were traitors to their own side. One such example was William J. Boyle, a private in the First New York Mounted Rifles. Boyle was part of a group of Union soldiers harassing some Williamsburg women near their encampment in Market Square. Lieutenant Disosway, his superior officer, rushed from the Palmer House down to their tents. Upon arrival, he reprimanded them and ordered them to be confined to their tents. A drunken Private Boyle grew angry and shot Disosway; the mortally wounded Lieutenant was carried back to the Palmer House. The Union doctor could do nothing for the wounded man, and he died several hours later. Boyle was tried, convicted of murder, and sentenced to death. A presidential order had recently been given putting a moratorium (legal authorization for a period of delay) on military executions, and a guard let Boyle escape. Boyle went straight to the Confederates in Richmond and gave up military secrets in exchange for his safety; in particular of an immanent cavalry attack with plans to free all Union prisoners-of-war at Belle Island and Libby Prison. The attack was stopped well before it reached Richmond with a well-prepared force at Bottom's Bridge; instead of releasing any Union prisoners, the cavalry lost a lot of men, angering officers in command.

The Gentleman Ghost

While Boyle escaped death in Williamsburg, Disosway did not, and some residents of the Palmer House insist that they have seen him. The gentleman Lieutenant, who always tried to prevent his men from abusing the civilian population—particularly the women—is now a gentleman ghost. He has been seen smoking a pipe while reading and has even smiled at the residents who have seen him.

After many attempts trying to find a paranormal presence over the Palmer House, I found a red super cell on the side, out for the full moon. Soon after, I found a mist-like apparition hovering in the trees near a second story window. Finally I found several male faces in the front windows at dusk one day. One face has a very full mustache and possibly a goatee—a style very much in vogue from the mid-nineteenth century till the start of the twentieth. A second photo is of a gap-mouthed young man who could have lived in any century, and the third photo is of a man who appears to be sleeping. He has no mustache, but he may have a beard—or just some distortion/grain from the photo. It's very possible that either the first or the third face could be that of the slain Lieutenant Disosway; I wonder if either of these faces is that of the gentleman officer who is seen quietly reading and smoking a pipe?

Here is the side of the house facing the Capitol, with an apparition that looks as if it's forming a human shape outside the window.

Is this the face of the lieutenant, the gentleman ghost that was shot in the back by one of his men? He looks out the front window of the Palmer House . . .

Here's another paranormal resident of the Palmer House, perhaps a young man who lived here or one of the very young soldiers (or drummer boys) fighting for the Union or the Confederacy.

Finally, just like the Prentis Store from the first book,
the Palmer House has what appears to be a sleeping
ghost—or perhaps that's how he looked when he died
. . .

THE PETER HAY APOTHECARY AND KITCHEN

The Glowing Red Eyes

History

A rebus marks the site of the Peter Hay Apothecary—an eighteenth-century drugstore. A *rebus* is a sign that is like a picture/puzzle meant for the largely illiterate population in that time period. Someone in that era may not be able to read the words Peter Hay Apothecary, but seeing the haystack on the sign would immediately let locals know that this was the site of Dr. Hay's drugstore (apothecary). Dr. Hay started his business here in 1740, and ran a successful and profitable business for sixteen years. A ferocious fire ended Hay's successful run in 1756. According to one newspaper report, the fire rapidly consumed the shop, so that within one-half hour everything was in ashes. The only thing that prevented the fire from spreading to any of the nearby buildings was the deployment of a fire engine—if you recall, by the mid-eighteenth century, Colonial Williamsburg had a fire engine housed in a shed on the side of the guardhouse—although quite primitive by today's standards.

The kitchen, a separate building right behind the apothecary, must have burned too, although the historical record is not clear. But perhaps the paranormal evidence might reveal what the public record or history does not. The rebuilt kitchen is a lodging house for tourists who want more of an eighteenth-century experience; however, some of them get a little something extra in their Williamsburg stay: a paranormal experience. Some have reported seeing an African-American slave, with bandages on his head and glowing red eyes, on the stairway of the kitchen. I can't confirm that story, but I can say with certainty that there are several apparitions that reside at the kitchen.

Overhead is a red super cell in miniature, very similar to the one at the Ewing House from the first book. As I said before, I don't know if a smaller apparition than normal means anything, because I've seen apparitions change in a matter of seconds from a small size to enormous. The apparition seen is that of a full-grown man, and not a child, so the size of the red super cell may have nothing to do with whether the person died as a child or as an adult. So the question that bears asking is what determines the size of an apparition—if not the size of the person, does it have to do with the size of one's intellect?

Below the miniature red super cell, at the back of the kitchen, I have captured the apparition with the glowing eyes—perhaps a frightening sight for those tourists having a temporary stay at the Hay Kitchen—but for me, an incredible find! Since this apparition was right below the red super cell in miniature, I had to wonder if the two were linked. In other words, was the apparition with the glowing eyes, as I have hypothesized before, a kind of hologram created by the entity that is the red super cell?

Like the tiny Slaves' Quarters from the first book, this petite building housed a plethora of wraiths besides the slave with the glowing eyes. A photo from the street side (front) of the building shows an odd assortment of phantoms at the kitchen, the most bizarre being a little girl resembling a doll—or was it a doll that held a spirit? I have seen "haunted dolls" before—could this be the apparition of a haunted doll? I cannot say for sure; what I can say is that bizarre apparitions are the "norm" in the paranormal paradigm!

Is this perhaps the man with the glowing red eyes that haunts the Peter Haye Kitchen? Unlike the story, this apparition does not have a bandaged head . . .

This is the Peter Hay Apothecary, and as you can see, it has its own apparition, but there are no known explanations or ghost stories that I could find.

These two faces appear to be twins, but one face is light and the other is dark.

I'm at a loss for this one: There's no legend or ghost story to explain the presence of this very young girl and the two classic whites; this is just bizarre . . .

This close-up of a single windowpane in the Peter Hay Apothecary has a face with no story—at least one that is known today. We have the different colored eyes again—each looking in a different direction. How's this for a very different look from the other faces; it appears as if it's spewing fire from its mouth.

JOHN COKE OFFICE

The Phantom Owl

History

Right next to Shield's Tavern is the John Coke office, an early nineteenth-century keeper of the Raleigh Tavern, which is across the street. There were two John Cokes in Williamsburg; this is most likely the office of John Coke II, the grandson of John Coke, a successful goldsmith who you may recall built the house next to the jail (gaol) where the president of the Colonial Williamsburg Foundation resides. The first John Coke arrived in 1724, from England, trying to escape a troubled youth. The second John Coke married the widow of James Shields III (James Shields II died in 1750, and John Coke II was born in 1762). Not much else is known about Coke or his office; perhaps the "troubled youth" moniker was placed on more than one member of the Coke family. Whether it was the Cokes or other residents, there is a lot of paranormal activity over this small, partially reconstructed eighteenth-century building.

The Owl

This may not have anything to do with the John Coke Office, but since the phantom owl was captured overhead, I thought it appropriate to link the story to it. But one apparition that I finally captured has been haunting—or perhaps taunting me through-out some of my nights trolling the deserted streets of Colonial Williamsburg.

Sometime in April, I began my evening journey at the Bruton Parish Church, site of my first success in this paranormal odyssey. I was planning to pass by the old house of worship, because I had plenty of photos of all the apparitions overhead and inside. As I came upon Bruton, I heard an owl that sounded like it was somewhere on the upper part of the steeple; as the nocturnal bird hooted I strained my eyes to see if I could spot it. I took several photos to see if it would show up—and it did not. I have never heard an owl call so persistently in such an urban area; and the sound clearly came from the front area of the church facing the Duke of Gloucester Street. I moved on, a bit puzzled by the anomaly, but nevertheless anxious to move on to the other houses and buildings I wanted to photograph. Somewhere between a quarter- and a half-mile away, I stopped at the Peyton Randolph House to hopefully discover another one of the many apparitions that seem to haunt this house.

The second that I stopped, I heard the same owl voice hooting from the large tree to the left front of Peyton's possessed domicile. The bird's voice emanated from the area by the upstairs far-left window—the location of the demonic eyes. So what was I to think: coincidence or creepy? Happenstance or haunting? I couldn't help but feel a little of each, as I made my way down the road to the jail, stopping briefly at the Tayloe House to capture a white pillar in the upstairs window. A few seconds after I arrived at the last residence of Blackbeard's crew, I heard a familiar voice. Okay, we have officially left the realm of chance and now arrived at the unnerving fact that the owl is following me, and a cold chill meandered down my spine.

From the gaol, I walked up the path to the Secretary's Office, and as I photographed the one-story brick building, the owl began to hoot from a tree to my right in the courtyard of the Capitol. I could still hear the owl nearby as I photographed the Palmer House and the Nicolson Store. At this point, I really felt eerily uncomfortable and decided I would leave. As I walked further down the Duke of Gloucester Street, I heard the owl at both the Philip Ludlow House as I passed as well as back at the Bruton Parish Church. The same thing happened several other times as I strode the streets of Williamsburg late at night, leaving me with an unsettling feeling about the unknown. My biggest fear was that it would follow me home, but thankfully that did not happen.

The night that I photographed the John Coke Office I was only in town for a few minutes before I went off to other sites outside of Williamsburg. I could see the red super cells around the office in the photos that I took, but one thing had evaded my attention because it was too small to see in the viewfinder: There was a small owl in the tree overhead. Here's the rub: Owls have large, dark eyes, and their pupils are usually opened very wide at night. This owl had large glowing eyes with small pupils; its undercarriage likewise had a glow about it—too high in the tree to be reflecting light from an artificial source. Could this be the wraith owl that had followed me throughout Colonial Williamsburg, making its presence known at every stop?

Seeing some of the other shapes and forms that these apparitions have taken on, it's not beyond the realm of possibility for them to take on the shape of an animal—is it? As the

Although this is a partial reconstruction, the John Coke Office has a very strong paranormal presence.

owl hooted, I was able to capture it on camera, for some reason certain that it was of the same voice that had followed me around Williamsburg, and it left me wondering—was it really an owl, or a wraith that appeared as an owl? I would later capture three different faces in the windows of this small office building, and my thoughts go immediately back to the owl. Could one of these faces have been responsible for the ghost owl? Could one of these faces create the apparition of an owl just as it created the apparition of their former self?

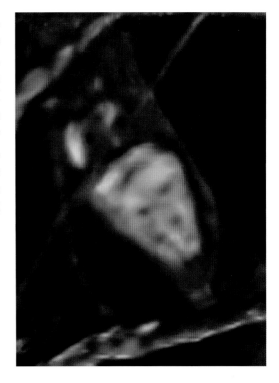

Is this an owl apparition with unnaturally glowing eyes? Is this the wraith that followed me around Williamsburg on several different occasions, hooting in a nearby tree at every stop?

 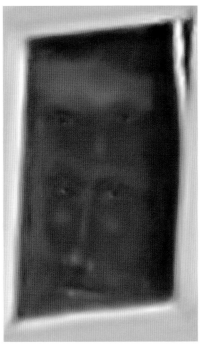 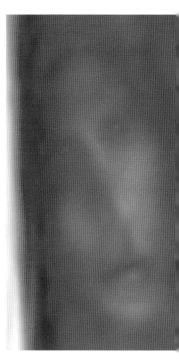

These four faces showed up inside this tiny office building on another night.

PRENTIS HOUSE

William Prentis:
The Protector or the Poltergeist?

History of a Businessman Ahead of His Time

Williams Prentis was born in 1699, in London, the same year that the Capitol moved from Jamestown to the newly created city of Williamsburg. His mother died about nine years later, and he was placed in the school at Christ's Hospital, the same orphanage that Thomas Everard was placed in at the age of ten. Like Everard, Prentis was taught accounting and business acumen at the school and was sent to America to be indentured to Archibald Blair for seven years. Prentis was only fourteen when he arrived in the New World with no family (Everard was sixteen), and he would remain in the service of Dr. Blair till his twenty-first birthday. Blair had gone into business with his brother, the Rev. James Blair (founder of the College of William and Mary), and Philip Ludwell (the father of Mad Lucy Ludwell from the first book). When Dr. Blair died in 1733, one of his daughters sold her one-sixth share of the store to Prentis, and William began a successful career as a store manager, as well as part owner of the Blair-Prentis-Cary store, which was soon renamed William Prentis and Co.

William Prentis married Mary Brooke, and his father-in-law gave him part of a lot that he owned, complete with a house, a stable, and a shed in 1725. John Brooke, the father-in-law, acquired the property in 1712, and had the home built on it in two years, using the

building as an ordinary (eighteenth-century version of a bed and breakfast). William and Mary (heard that name before?) had six children, with John being the oldest and heir to both the house and his father's shares of the store he managed.

In 1740, a new, larger brick store (still standing) replaced the older frame building to the east. Not only had Prentis expanded the store's area, but also he built a building out of brick (a much more expensive endeavor) to cater to Williamsburg's elite. Prentis was ahead of his time for an eighteenth-century business, for some of the practices he introduced included stockholder meetings, annual financial statements, published results of the meetings, financial incentives to management, and reinvestment of earnings. Prentis also served as justice of the peace for many years, starting in 1734, and he died in 1765. He had accumulated one of the largest personal fortunes in Williamsburg, and was buried in the floor of the Bruton Parish Church.

The Virginia Tea Party

John Prentis, born in 1753, took over the reigns of his father's store in 1765, and the stressful times leading up to the Revolution may have shortened the entrepreneur's life. John ignored the non-importation agreement for English goods in 1774, having two half-chests of tea shipped to Yorktown to be brought to his Williamsburg store. The Yorktown residents discovered the tea shipment, and the irate citizens tossed Prentis' tea into the York River—so Boston wasn't the only place where tea was thrown overboard into the river! Virginians were so angry about this *faux pas* that Prentis had to write a profound apology in the *Virginia Gazette* so the people of Williamsburg would not boycott his store. John already had a miserable home life—married to a woman who was insane—and between coping with his wife's insanity and the troubles from importing English tea, John would die just a year later.

A committee was appointed to manage John's estate, since his wife, Elizabeth, was of "unsound mind," and his brother, Daniel, would rent the house until he became owner from 1783 to 1796, when the physical Prentis presence ended in the house on Duke of Gloucester Street, which would burn in 1842. But the presence of William Prentis continues in the reconstructed house that Colonial Williamsburg built.

Protector of Children

A while back one of the vice-presidents of Colonial Williamsburg moved into the Prentis House, and this woman had two children. The first night that they stayed there, the children could not go to sleep because there was a man in colonial dress who was standing at the doorway to their room, and he was watching them—and by the way, he fit the description of William Prentis from a painting of him. Somehow they made it through the night, and gradually the kids got used to the apparition. What they realized is that the ghost was not watching them, but watching over them—like a protector. Since I have photographed more than one ghost there, it is possible that he was protecting them from other entities in the

house, possibly even from the insane spirit of Elizabeth, the wife of William's son, John. It got to the point that the children realized that William was looking out for them, and they could not go to sleep *without seeing their protector at the doorway*.

The Poltergeist?

I covered the Prentis Store in my first book, but I learned of this true story from Colonial Williamsburg Security. Several women entered the Prentis store (which is a functioning store), and one began to comment loudly on how everything was ridiculously over-priced. A poltergeist flung a chessboard displayed on the wall across the room and hit the woman in the face—hard enough that the woman had a gash in her face and had to be taken to the hospital to have her wound stitched up. In my musings, I have wondered whether a ghost could be in two places at the same time, or did another ghost initiate the attack—possibly one of William Prentis' sons who ran the store after William died? Could William be both the protector of children and the poltergeist? Is that the dichotomy of one personality, or is it impossible for one ghost to haunt two different locations? I have heard of Abraham Lincoln's ghost haunting four different locations; is that even possible? I guess the only way that I could prove it to myself and you is if I could capture the same wraith at two different locations—and so far, I haven't been able to do that, but I will keep trying.

I found a variety of faces in the Prentis House, including some bearded faces that appear to be circa the Civil War. There are a couple of female faces that make me wonder if John Prentis' insane wife, Elizabeth, is still on the premises. The final two faces look very similar to each other, and one of the people that have rented the Prentis House from Colonial Williamsburg has witnessed the angry stare from a ghost—is this the face that he saw? The face seems unusually long, and in both cases, for some strange reason, is missing the mouth. The first photo was taken on a dark moonless night of the front of the house, the second on a brightly lit night (with a full moon) of the side of the house. If you notice, I show the second photo of the side view of the Prentis House because you can plainly see one of the two faces in a windowpane on the lower right—the whole pane is glowing white with the eyes and nose of the face plainly visible from the street. Evidently this ghost wants to be seen!

This is the side view of the Prentis House on the night of a full moon, and you can see a glowing face in one of the windowpanes to the lower right side.

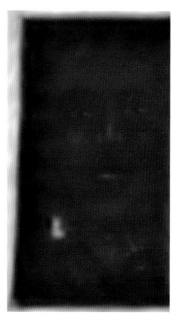

Here's a man with a full beard, and I'm inclined to think he is from right before the Civil War era.

Here's a couple of faces that appeared in a nearby windowpane; I don't think they have spiked hair—I think those are other apparitions trying to appear.

Here's a ghost with a rather pleasant look on her face accompanied by a bearded man below. I haven't seen very many happy faces in this dimension . . .

A female apparition, which makes me wonder if she is the insane wife of John Prentis . . .

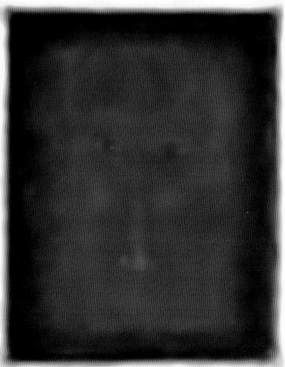

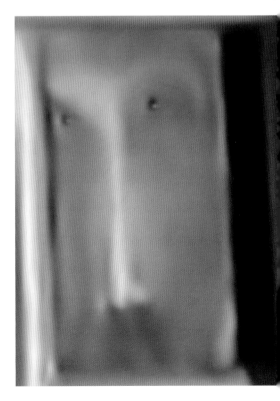

I captured these two faces on two separate nights; the first on a dark, moonless night in front of the house, and the second on a bright moonlit night on the side of the house. They both have the same long nose and glaring eyes—is it the same ghost?

PARTY ON THE DUKE OF GLOUCESTER STREET

You've Heard of the After Party—How about the After-Life Party?

I had been concentrating on finding ghosts in the houses, but finding a second and third apparition in the corner of the photo of the Taliaferro Cole House made me think that I should go back and check all the photographs that I had taken to make sure that I had not missed anything in the far corners of the photo, and am I glad I did! When I looked back at the Roscow Cole House, I found something amazing in the far left corner of the photograph: A gathering of ghosts! As I write this (in mid-January 2014) there is all of this spin about award shows (such as the Golden Globes, Grammys, Oscars), and one of the questions directed to the celebrities is: Whose after-party are you going to? I wonder if they know that evidently ghosts have parties too.

On a cold evening in March, with hardly any traffic in Colonial Williamsburg, I went on one of my treks through this living museum to find the dead. I always check around me to make sure that a tourist or a tavern worker does not ruin my photo by walking in front of my camera. Once I had determined that the coast was clear, I took several shots of the Roscow Cole House. The first photo was pure magic, and in all of the following photographs all of the ghosts disappeared, except for the electric-blue fountain-shaped apparition I had captured over the house. It's as if I had disturbed their party, and they vanished in a split second! Although I have enough images in this one photo to write a mini-book on ghosts, I've only chosen to put the clearest and most interesting of the lot in this chapter.

One other thing that I discovered was something that I did not expect: Not all of the ghosts here are from the Colonial or Civil War period. The first phantom to catch my attention was what appeared to be the back of a woman in blue jeans with a white top, who seems to be looking across the street at the after-life party. (I know, it's only logical to expect ghosts from any time period.) Accompanying her is at least one, if not two ghosts that are barely there, just a white wisp of light. Across the street is what appears to be the combination of a woman in antebellum (or is it Victorian?) attire with a featureless grey face. Behind this woman is a gathering of what appears to be Native American faces, perhaps from another century or even time period. In the farthest left corner of the photograph is a misty, ephemeral gathering of ghosts that appear to be around a table. In and around the trees were a host of faces that were somewhere in the netherworld between humanity and the edge of our comprehension. Finally, there was a couple dressed in late nineteenth-century attire who were relaxing on a bench—a bench that was not there when they were alive! That spring night there seemed to be an awakening of the ghosts; perhaps they were all out celebrating the end of winter. Whatever the after-life party was commemorating, I was overjoyed that I stumbled upon their world—even if it was only for one frame.

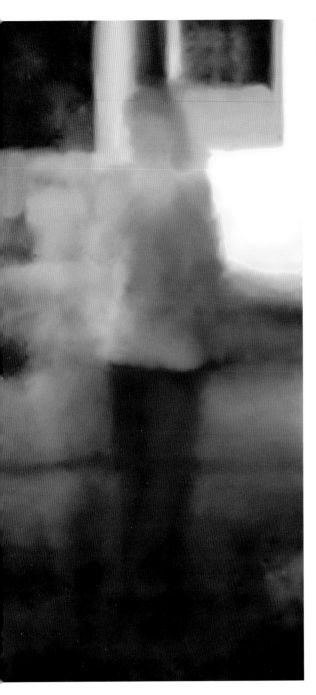

This woman with a featureless face is across the street from the previous apparition. Note the high-neck collar, perhaps Victorian, and is that a skull forming on her shoulder?

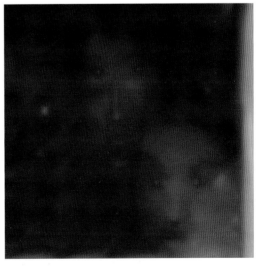

The ghost of a woman in blue jeans is not what I expected to find in Colonial Williamsburg, along with one or two white wispy wraiths.

This is a crop of the first close-up so that you could see the apparitions forming across the street over top a fence. Two partial faces with glowing eyes that appear more than a little menacing accompany two full and yet innocuous faces. Many who have seen this photo believe the faces to be Native America; what do you think?

Okay, I made you wait for it; now here it is: Depending on what you count, there are at least seven or more shapes in this ghostly gathering across the Duke of Gloucester Street from the Roscow Cole House. The person standing to the far right, like the first person in blue jeans, also appears to be wearing fairly modern clothing . . . perhaps the first time a party of the paranormal has been captured on film?

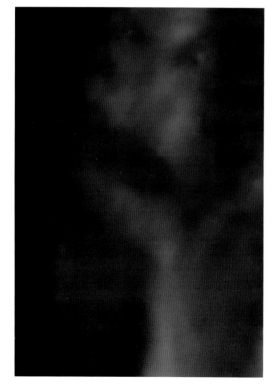

Have you ever seen the manufactured faces that you can purchase and nail to your tree? Well here's the real deal: one of many faces to appear on the trunk of this large tree next to the Roscow Cole House.

This is the second of quite a few apparitions that I found in the trees in the photo; although this seems to be a formidable phantom, this angry apparition is really quite small. I found this in foliage of the tree across the street.

Check out this evanescent couple sitting on a
bench. Victorian fashion perhaps?

WILLIAMSBURG THEATER

Brother versus Brother

The first planned shopping center in the United States is what is today known as Merchant Square, built for the restored Colonial Williamsburg. It was a shopping center to serve the needs of the workers for the newly created Colonial Williamsburg Foundation, as well as all of the tourists who would visit America's first "living museum." Besides the basic needs of employees and visitors, Rockefeller planned to fill some of the entertainment needs by building a theater in the square, appropriately named the "Williamsburg Theater." The theater opened in 1933, appropriately enough performing the first play to be put on in British North America: George Farquhar's Restoration Comedy *The Recruiting Officer*, shown of course in Williamsburg. The theater underwent a much-needed restoration in the year 2000, and was renamed the Kimball Theatre in honor of the family who financed the remodel. But to understand the haunting of the theater, you must go back in time to the house that was originally built on the same ground.

The theater sat on the site of a home owned by the Ware family. During the Civil War, the Battle of Williamsburg (Fort Magruder), Confederate wounded from the battle were taken into individual homes, because the makeshift hospitals were overflowing (the Bruton Parish Church, Market Square Tavern, Coke-Garrett House . . .). The women of the Ware family took on the care of a severely wounded young Rebel soldier, who despite their best efforts died. They laid him out in the parlor, awaiting an appropriate burial, when the Confederate Army retreated to Richmond. The Union Army took over Williamsburg, and sent soldiers from door to door looking for wounded Confederate soldiers. A Union soldier showed up at the Ware home and was escorted to the parlor, and pointed towards the body of the young Rebel soldier who was covered with a sheet. The blue-clad Union soldier pulled back the sheet, and immediately began to weep: The Civil War not only divided the country, it divided families, and he discovered that the deceased Confederate under the sheet was his brother. The grieving Union soldier would soon die for the cause that divided his family, and he came back postmortem to the site of his brother's death to look for him: A man clad in a navy-blue uniform is seen searching the backrooms of the theater frantically—and then abruptly disappears from sight. As you will soon see, this story may account for two of the apparitions overhead, but there are more at the front of the building. In the exterior windows I found bearded faces that are probably from the Civil War—could one or two of these be the brothers who decided to fight on opposite sides of the conflict? One specter has quite a different look—is he perhaps one of the cast of performers from the past?

The former Williamsburg Theater, renamed The Kimball Theatre in honor of the family who financed its 2000 restoration, has a host of apparitions hovering overhead.

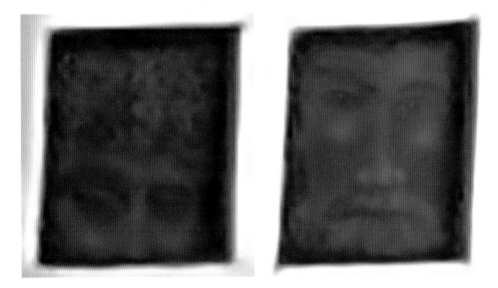

These apparitions looked down upon me from the second story of The Kimball Theatre. A Union soldier has been seen inside the back rooms frantically searching for his dead brother—who fought for the Confederacy. Could any of these apparitions be the two brothers—or perhaps more soldiers?

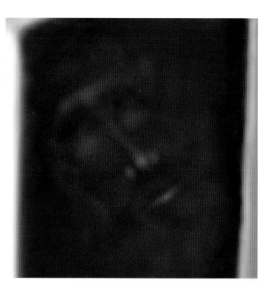

What appears to be the same apparition followed me from the front to the side window; he also appears to be from the Civil War.

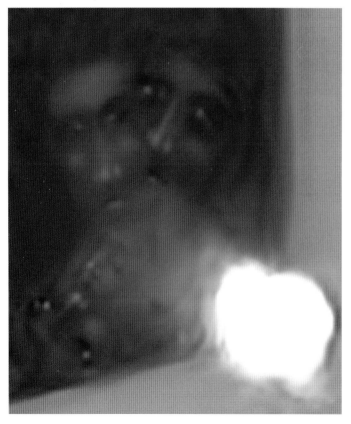

This group of faces appeared on the inside of the building in the window of the room where all of the theater's equipment and film projectors reside.

TRAVIS HOUSE

Irremovable Blood Stain

The Travis House is one that was built about 1765, by Edward Champion Travis, Colonel of the James City County Militia and a member of the Virginia House of Burgesses representing James City County. Since he did not live in Williamsburg, this house was most likely a tenement (rental property). As I mentioned before, many Southern families would use the same first name from father to son to grandson to great-grandson without adding Sr., Jr., or numbers after the name; this seems to be the case for Edward Travis, who happened to be the fourth in line. But although Colonial Williamsburg has named this home for Travis, the most interesting, compelling story came from the superintendent in charge of the Eastern Lunatic Asylum.

Dr. John Minson Galt was the superintendent of the *Public Hospital for Persons of Insane and Disordered Minds* for twenty years when his term came to an abrupt and tragic end. (Before we go any further, you have to understand that only people with mental incapacities were placed in a hospital; sick or injured people were cared for at their homes, and the medical doctor would make house-calls; something unheard of today.)

Here is a little background information for the hospital Dr. Galt was in charge of: Long after the house passed from the Travis family's hands, it was purchased by the State of Virginia to be the superintendent's house for the mental hospital. Right across the street from the Travis House stands a reconstructed version of the first building in North America

built to treat the mentally ill, although in today's terms '*treat*' may be the wrong word for how the mentally incapacitated were dealt with. Construction began in 1771, and the first patient was admitted on October 12, 1773. If you recall from the first book, Mad Lucy Ludwell (Paradise) was the first female occupant of the hospital. (Remember the woman who had her expensive carriage assembled on her back porch, and took people for a "ride" back and forth the length of the porch?)

Dr. Galt was a special man, and before I tell you why he was special, let's look at how mental patients were treated prior to his tenure as superintendent of the Williamsburg Hospital. The building housed twenty-four cells that were reserved for either those who were deemed dangerous or those who were curable. Those considered harmless but incurable were not admitted. Each cell was equipped with a heavy door with a barred window that looked onto a dim central passage, a mattress, a chamber pot (eighteenth-century toilet, which I might add the contents could be ammunition in the wrong hands), and an iron ring in the wall to which the patient's wrist or leg fetters were attached. If you haven't grasped the idea yet, this facility was more for containment than treatment, and the tools used were the following: restraints, strong drugs, plunge baths and other "shock" water treatments, an electro-static machine, bleeding, and blistering salves. If that were not enough, two dungeon-like cells were dug out beneath the hospital in 1799, to house the patients in a *raving frenzy*. (Most places in

Williamsburg do not have basements because of the difficulty of keeping out water.)

By 1836, new ideas began to be instituted to replace imprisonment and chains: the "moral management" approach emphasized kindness, firm but gentle encouragement to self-control, work therapy, and leisure activity. Accompanying these changes patients were supplied with real beds and other comforts. One of the men who spearheaded this approach to mental illness was Dr. John Galt, a little-known pioneer for the modern psychiatric hospital, whose voice as an advocate for the insane was often ignored. Galt's ideas and treatments were at least one hundred years ahead of his time, and the hospital's Court of Directors would often stand in opposition to the progressive ideas of the pioneering doctor.

Galt, as you can probably tell, was a man devoted to his work and had not married but lived in the Travis House with his sister, Sarah, for more than twenty years. Death had been slowly taking its toll on the close-knit Galt family, with brother Alexander dead in his twenties, sister Elizabeth dead from a long illness, and then the mother in 1858. Sarah cared for the Travis House, now referred to as the Superintendent's House, while her brother took care of his patients in the hospital across the street—that is, until the Civil War came to Williamsburg.

By the outbreak of the War Between the States, the hospital had about 300 patients, a third story on the main building, and seven other buildings on the eight acres that the hospital occupied. The Civil War came to town on May 5, 1862, and was a major culture shock for the quiet farming community of Williamsburg. No longer the bustling capital of Virginia, the city had fewer than 2,000 residents, and now suddenly it had almost twice that number in dead soldiers. Yes, the dead and dying were everywhere in Williamsburg in the days following the inconclusive battle. Add to that

the Union-occupied Williamsburg for the duration of the war instituting marshal law on the townspeople, who considered the *Yankees* to be foreign aggressors. As part of the marshal law, the federal authorities did the unthinkable to Dr. John Galt—they denied him further entry to his beloved asylum and to his patients. The patient advocate for humane treatment was suddenly forbidden to continue with his life's pursuit, which was too much to bear for the devoted doctor. Less than two weeks after this decision was made, the good doctor could not see his life's work taken from him, and he overdosed on the drug *opiate laudanum*. The Union provost then told Galt's sister Sarah (known to many as "Sallie") that she had to leave her home of more than twenty years, the Superintendent's House, which added further grief to the devastated woman.

Now in addition to all of the aforementioned things that disrupted the lives of people living in Williamsburg, I am going to add one more item, although I do so with a caution: I cannot find the original source. One of the things not mentioned in Colonial Williamsburg's records of the Public Hospital or on the Eastern State website is another atrocity committed by the Union army. They set all the patients in the asylum free to wander the city and countryside—something that may have been what propelled Dr. Galt to commit suicide. I have looked and continue to look with diligence as to whether this is a fact of the Union occupation; what I do know is that I read it in a personal account of the Civil War in Williamsburg.

The Supernatural Bloodstain and the Ghosts

Dr. Galt's death is a tragedy that continues in the way of a bloodstain on the wooden floors of the old Travis House. Shortly after the Galts left the Superintendent's House, the Lee family moved in. Mrs. Lee's personal experience:

I could do nothing to get the blood stain out of the floorboards. No amount of scrubbing would remove it. We finally had to pull up the soiled portion and replace it with fresh wood. I was shocked to find the very next morning, the stain somehow made its way onto the new flooring! . . . My children are frightened. They wake me most every night claiming a man is in the upstairs room where Doctor Galt died.

I do not know if the actual overdose caused the doctor to bleed, or if he fell after taking the overdose and hit his head, causing the irremovable bloodstain, but I do find it incredible that a ghost can recreate a bloodstain on the new wood put down.

After reading about Dr. Galt, his commitment to his patients, his devotion to his job, and the fact that he was at least one hundred years ahead of his peers in treating the mentally ill, I would not think that his ghost would engage in making all of the paranormal noise that has been heard in the house. But then again, there are more than enough photos of the possible poltergeists. Which one do you think may be Dr. Galt? Which one do you think is responsible for all the noise? I can't help but wonder if the noisy ghost is a former resident of the asylum across the street . . .

Here's a view of the Travis House from across the street in the lot of the first hospital built (and now rebuilt) in North America for people with mental illness. One of the upstairs bedrooms has the irremovable blood stain . . .

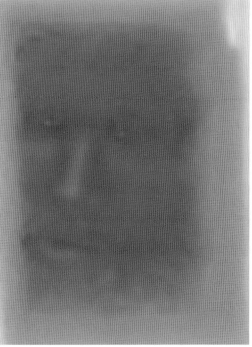

This is one of two apparitions that I thought might be Dr. John Minson Galt, the superintendent of the public hospital across the street.

Or could this apparition be Dr. Galt, the man who committed suicide in the upstairs bedroom when the Union army forbade him from seeing his patients?

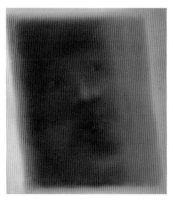

I've seen this before at the Wythe House—an eye appears in the mouth of this apparition—is this enough to keep you up at night?

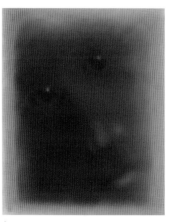

This apparition appears to be too young to be the suicidal doctor—perhaps a child that died in this house?

These three ghosts look alien-like; what do you think about that possibility? Or is it just an incomplete human face?

RETURN TO WILLIAM AND MARY

Alma Mater of a Nation of the Living . . .
and the Dead

The College of William and Mary is known as the "Alma Mater of a Nation" because of its close ties to the founding fathers. George Washington received his surveyor's license through the college at the age of seventeen, and he would become its first American chancellor. Thomas Jefferson received his undergraduate education here, and studied law under George Wythe, who would become the first professor of law at the nation's first law school—at William and Mary. In fact, George Wythe signed a very important document written by his prodigious pupil: Thomas Jefferson's Declaration of Independence. Presidents James Monroe and John Tyler also got their undergraduate degrees here. The ghosts of none of these men are thought to be here, but there is a plethora of apparitions with some great stories about their presumed identities.

I photographed William and Mary's "ancient campus" in the first book, which includes the three buildings that were built in the late 1600s–early 1700s: The Wren Building (1695), the Brafferton (1723), and the President's House (1732). Since then I've had reason to return to some of the buildings on the "old campus," the Crim Dell, (a small pond on the William and Mary campus) and the Phi Beta Kappa Memorial Hall: Do I need to say it? There are more ghost stories associated with these places and more ghost portraits to be taken—whether it be the colored geometric light formations (geo-light for short), the classic white Halloween ghost (classic white for short), or the actual representation of their

former selves. My first stop was the first building to be constructed on the "old campus," which is right behind the Wren building: Tucker Hall.

Tucker Hall was finished and dedicated in 1909, as the college's new library. It was financed by Andrew Carnegie, whose endowment fund would later double the library's size in 1922. Then the library was moved to a new building (Earl Greg Swem Library) and the building went under renovation to become the law school in 1967, officially renamed the Marshall-Wythe Hall in 1968, to honor both George Wythe and another of the school's famous alumni, John Marshall, who become the first chief justice of the Supreme Court. In 1980, the law school moved to a new building off the old campus, and it became the home of the English department. At that point, the building was renamed "Tucker Hall," in honor of St. George Tucker (remember his house from the first book?), the lawyer/law professor and a veteran of the Revolutionary War. When questioned if the ghost in Tucker Hall could be St. George Tucker himself, a research historian for Colonial Williamsburg said that Tucker was "as dull as dishwater," and that he would make one boring ghost.

As it turns out, this is not a lackluster ghost, and *she* has made *her* presence known in a number of innovative, intelligent, and frightening ways. Yes, it is a female ghost, and she is presumed to have committed suicide on the third floor of Tucker Hall in 1980. Some stories say a third-floor classroom, some say specifically room 301, and others say the third-floor bathroom was the site of the tragedy. Perhaps most frightening about this story is a suicide several years later by another young female student in the same spot, accompanied by the handwritten note: "She made me do it!"

In October 2004, a third suicide occurred in Tucker Hall—this time a male student. Whether he left a note blaming the influence of the first suicide is not known, but what *is* known is a story about the original female student told by both students and alumni: An unknown female student appears to other students who are studying for exams in Tucker Hall. Evidently, her appearance is quite ordinary and not like a ghostly apparition, so students are not alarmed when the ghost inquires how their study for the finals is coming along. If a student responds to the question in a positive way, saying that he or she feels good about finals, the answer triggers a violent response from the unstable female inquirer: She smashes her hands against walls and windows in a fit of rage until the intimidated students leave the building. Students and professors in Tucker Hall have witnessed other activities attributed to this unstable specter: windows opening on their own, a sound like "fingernails scratching a blackboard," and footsteps on the third floor late at night—minus the person making them. Just look at the following photos for visual proof of multiple wraiths at Tucker Hall . . .

Technology Savvy Ghosts?

There is another story that is attributed to the Tucker Hall ghost, one that was covered in the news from the English Department, dated March 16, 2006. This is twenty-six years after the suicide of the female student who purportedly haunts Tucker Hall. In this article, two students were working on a film project in Tucker Hall late one evening. The film, which had been completed the previous spring, was on a macabre subject: *Frankenstein: Penetrating the Secrets of Nature*. The two students who took on this independent study project did not realize how much of their time the project would consume. So when they came back to school the next fall, they wanted to complete the last part of their assignment as quickly as possible: Convert and burn fifteen DVDs and distribute them to the "people involved in the exhibit." They went to the Tucker Hall film editing room in the basement to finish the project rapidly, but something was causing their computer to crash—and the last time the computer would not turn back on. So the two left for an hour and came back with the hope that the computer would convert their film to the format they needed. They were elated to find that upon their return, the computer both turned on and converted their film. They both watched the film to make sure there were no problems or defects, and when satisfied that the film was ready, they began to burn the film to DVD. At 2:00 a.m. they finished the last DVD, and one of the students insisted that they watch it just to be sure. They were both shocked and dismayed to find strange effects and footage that was not even taken in their film—nor was it on the computer! They discovered, among other things, black-and-white footage of children reading, "the image of a Spanish dancer in a long dress, and extreme close-ups of some of our classmates' mouths." They had heard of the Tucker Hall ghost story before, but this was their first experience with a ghost of any type.[1] This ghost died before this technology was invented—how did she master it well enough to both bring in content from the Internet, create new film footage, and then insert it into their film file? Do the ghosts have to learn this technology, or do they immediately assimilate it from the minds of the people around them?

I ask these questions because of my own experience with a ghost at the Elkanah Dean House that I related in the first book. My sister, like myself someone who doubted the existence of ghosts, expressed her doubts out loud to the rest of us as we walked to the front of the house. She brought her iPhone to take photos, and immediately began to ask me why she could not see the house as she held the iPhone up facing the Dean House. She had the camera app on, but rather than seeing the house when she held the iPhone up, you could see in grainy black and white what we discovered to be the ghost of a man—who was in the iPhone but not visible to any of us! So here is another case—my sister had just bought the iPhone and was quite unsure of the technology, but the ghost was able to make itself show up on her screen. This man had very dated clothing— he could have died a hundred years ago, and yet he was literally inside the iPhone looking at us. Do they have the ability to instantly master our technology, no matter when they died? Although I don't know how, from what I've seen personally, I can't help but think that they can. I've seen a ghost take over a photography app on an iPhone, and two students from William and Mary have seen a ghost take over film-editing and conversion software and create scenes that were not even in the original film; how advanced is that? If someone introduced me to technology invented one hundred years from now, I believe that it would take a while for me to master it—I might even have to take a class on it. At the same time, I think of something that I have heard over and over in conversation: We only use ten percent of our brain's capability. Do these creatures have one hundred percent of their mental processing faculty, whatever that is, and do they have the ability to quickly

assimilate and even master any of our technology? Can they process anything ten times faster than we can at any given moment? This capability is mind-boggling, especially if they were once one of us . . .

I visited the "old campus" quite a few times, but it was my final visit, on a late-December full moon, with record-breaking warm temperatures, that I captured the faces in and around Tucker Hall, the beautiful, but primarily ultraviolet light geo-lights inside the Phi Beta Kappa Hall's theater, and the strange apparitions in the waters of the Crim Dell. I wonder how many students, or even professors, realize that they are sharing their learning/teaching experience with ghosts . . . perhaps the phantoms are sitting in the classroom with them . . .

On the "old campus," the Tucker Hall ghost is the only one that is talked about in the college newspaper, the *Flat Hat,* as well as on the campus itself. We're going to look at a few of the apparitions I've captured in

Here is the apparition at Tucker Hall that may be the specter of a female student who committed suicide in 1980.

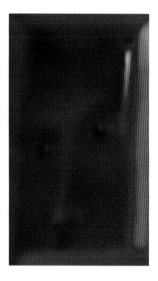

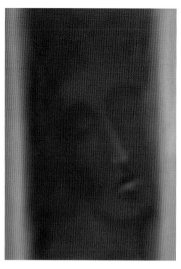

One of the ghosts at Tucker Hall; could this be the male student who committed suicide, or is it another student or professor from the building and/or ground's past?

Another face in the Tucker Hall gallery: Is this the same ghost that flies into a rage when she hears that other students are doing well on their finals?

A complete face on the right is offset by a stacking apparition on the left—indicative that Tucker has more than a few paranormal presences.

and around Tucker Hall; could one of these faces in the windows be the ghost that tries to intimidate students studying for finals? I will leave you be the judge of that; but I've discovered that every building on the old campus has its own ghosts. Although I do not have stories to go with all these ghosts, I can prove to you that they exist. I will only show you several of the best photos, as some apparitions are very difficult to see through the trees. One of the most intriguing photos was that of two youthful apparitions standing by a tree near the front of Tucker Hall, one a gap-mouthed young man seen from the torso up that I would guess was a former student; see what you think . . .

Phi Beta Kappa Memorial Hall

Supposedly, one of the reasons for a haunting is unfinished business. That certainly seems to be the case at the Phi Beta Kappa Memorial Hall. The unfinished business was a play, stranger still, a play whose integral characters include ghosts: Thornton Wilder's *Our Town*. Back in the 1950s, a student named Lucinda had the lead part in the play, but two weeks before opening night she died in a car crash. The show went on without Lucinda—her understudy (replacement) took over Lucinda's role. One evening, as Lucinda's understudy practiced the play alone in the theater, she looked out into the audience to see the white dress that she was to wear for the play sitting upright in a seat in the balcony. On opening night, during a graveyard scene, the replacement looked out into the audience and saw the very student she replaced, Lucinda, sitting in the balcony—donning the black dress from the graveyard scene. According to the William and Mary theatrical department, she has not left. Every once in a while she makes her presence known: One time a student was practicing his part for the play on the piano; when he finished, he heard a voice

I captured these apparitions on the walkway coming towards Tucker Hall; perhaps more students from a parallel dimension.

exclaim, "Don't Stop!" When he got up to leave, evidently Lucinda punished him for not listening by turning the lights out in the building and locking him in the chamber pit. Lucinda is given credit for the broken pipe organ in the storage room playing by itself. Evidently, Lucinda doesn't like anyone to talk about her, because when they do she usually responds by creating a problem with the lighting or the sound system. (Another example of a ghost tampering with technology that did not exist when it was "alive," or should I say when it was human?) Lucinda's ghost has been spotted rather frequently, usually sitting in the balcony in one of the costumes from *Our Town*. A technical director

witnessed the apparition looking from a balcony window at him—black dress on and ready to resume her role in the play, even if the director was the only one in the auditorium. Although he second-guesses himself all the time about what he really saw, from the evidence I've collected I would say that he likely saw a ghost.

Did you notice that I did not say Lucinda? That's because I have evidence of not one but four or possibly more ghosts in Phi Beta Kappa Memorial Hall. The first photo I took of the exterior of the building, I found a spherical apparition overhead that morphed into a larger geo-light in the next photo. I was able to go inside the theater, and since no play was in

Here is a dominant spherical apparition overhead of the Phi Beta Kappa Memorial Hall—the College of William and Mary's Theater.

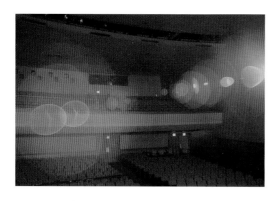

I photographed the deserted theater when there was only one floor lamp lit on the stage. Many geo-light apparitions showed up around the theater—primarily in ultraviolet light—including this one.

production at the time, I was able to take photographs. My interest was, of course, to take photos of the seats, focusing on the balcony, where Lucinda has been so frequently seen. The only window in the whole place was on the balcony—it was the light and sound room. So perhaps the supernatural activity in Phi Beta Kappa cannot all be blamed on Lucinda; she has accomplices—or fellow actors! I visited the theater a second time, and was surprised to discover that a lone floor lamp (something like what you would see in a living room, only without a lamp shade) that stood on the stage was the only light on in the theater. I captured four geo-light apparitions, appearing primarily in ultraviolet light, and several faces, each with their own facet of bizarre. I have my doubts if any may qualify as Lucinda, but you can make your own decision after seeing the photos.

Crim Dell

The Crim Dell is a small pond down the hill from the Sunken Gardens (not really a garden, just a grassy area between the buildings of the Old Campus where students gather to study, to picnic, or to throw a Frisbee.) The

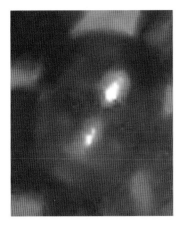

The faces that I captured at the Phi Beta Kappa Memorial Theater.

legend of the Crim Dell is really the lore of the Crim Dell Bridge: If you want a love that will last forever, go across the bridge with your lover and stop at the top for a kiss to seal your destiny. If you deny that destiny by breaking up, you will be forever cursed. If you want to break the curse, you must return to the bridge with your former lover, and from the top you must push the other off the bridge and into the pond. I broke the second legend of the Crim Dell Bridge several times to take photographs for this book: If you walk across the bridge alone, you (in this case "I") will be doomed to a life of loneliness. As for the second myth, I am anything but lonely, but the first one that I spoke of has something innately more dangerous than the fairy-tale curse on your life: Pushing someone off the top of the bridge may not only remove the curse, it just might kill him or her! A graduating student who had everything to live for is dying proof of that statement, so read on.

In 2003, a male student was the assistant director of orientation, a tour guide for the families of incoming students, a campus leader, a good student, a member of a fraternity, and a finalist to be a commencement speaker. This affable student decided to celebrate his upcoming graduation as well as his final tour of the campus by doing a back flip from the Crim Dell Bridge into the pond. He had an accomplice that not only knew ahead of time what he was about to do, but also pre-planned to be a part of this stunt: He would pull his coleader of the tour into the water with him when he performed his back flip. They both went into the water as arranged; she surfaced unharmed from the

Here is the Crim Dell and its beloved bridge, a gift to the college from the Class of 1964, from which a graduating senior foolishly did a life-ending back flip to celebrate his graduation and last tour. At the top of the bridge you can see a small hexagon-shaped orb accompanied by a bright yellow orb about the size of a softball—could that be him?

stunt, but he did not. Other students who witnessed the event began to jump into the pond to search the murky water for the submerged undergraduate. They found him and were able to pull him out of the Crim Dell and commence CPR, but he never regained consciousness. Paramedics were able to establish an irregular heartbeat on arrival, but thirty minutes after he reached the hospital he was pronounced dead. A young man who was just about to start his career and an independent life is gone—talk about unfinished business.

In addition to the graduating senior who met an untimely death doing a back flip into the Crim Dell, several other students have drowned in its dark, murky waters over the years. That doesn't take into account the unknown about this part of the campus: For example, during the Civil War the Wren Building was the point of demarcation between ground held by the Union forces and a no-man's-land between Williamsburg and Richmond. (Union soldiers burned the Wren Building because they thought Rebel sharpshooters were using it as cover to pick off Union soldiers. Then they bricked up all the windows facing west except for small gun portals—essentially using the

brick shell of the Wren Building as a fort for the remainder of the Civil War.) The Confederates regularly sent Calvary raids into Williamsburg, one time even capturing the commanding officer and hauling him off to a Confederate prison in Richmond. How many Rebel soldiers were shot in this area as they rode and/or marched into Williamsburg to conduct a raid? How many soldiers, students, and Native Americans died right around the area known as the Crim Dell, and how many of them are lost souls that still reside there?

When I photographed the bridge, I discovered a rather small hexagon-shaped orb right at the top center of the bridge, along with a softball-sized bright yellow orb, as well as beautiful geo-lights at each end over the lampposts. Were any of these the unfortunate senior? Finally, I discovered two apparitions right in the water, and for some reason one had a reflection, and one did not: Both apparitions had shapes I have not seen before, and the reflection anomaly has me puzzled: If digital light sensors can pick up the light—why can't the water reflect it? I don't know if one or any of these was that poor student with an unfinished life, but it sure felt like it . . .

By far, the most intriguing find at the Crim Dell so far has been these two apparitions in the water—even more puzzling—why does the apparition to the right have a reflection, and the one to the left has none?

FIRST AFRICAN AMERICAN CHURCH OF WILLIAMSBURG

The Ghost That Defies Description

History

African slaves who became converts to Christianity were the fruits of evangelical Presbyterians, Baptists, and Methodists, in the 1760s and 1770s. An itinerant black preacher named Moses came to town to teach Christianity to the slave population (about fifty-two percent of the general population), but "slave patrols" caught him meeting clandestinely with other slaves—which was against Virginia law—and the preacher was publicly whipped (according to the law) for up to thirty-nine lashes. Gowan Pamphlet, an enslaved tavern worker for Jane Vobe, who owned the King's Arm Tavern, decided to take up preaching when Moses left town. Some of Vobe's slaves learned how to read the Bible and write, and were allowed to take part in formal church services at Bruton Parish Church, and Gowan is presumed to be one of them. Vobe served the likes of William Byrd III, Sir Peyton Skipwith, and George Washington, and as a result, she trained her slaves in etiquette, manners, and the service of formal dinners.

Gowan heard his calling to be a preacher during a busy time for Jane Vobe's business; while officers from the Continental Army lodged and dined at the King's Arm Tavern, Gowan would negotiate for time off so that he could oversee his flock, who were meeting in secret at Green Spring plantation. By 1781, Gowan had about 200 followers in his congregation, meeting in a new wooded area south of Jamestown Road—and still in secret. When Virginia Governor Thomas Jefferson moved the capital to Richmond in 1780, the once bustling capital began to morph into a sleepy rural town, causing Jane Vobe to move her tavern to Chesterfield County, right across the James River from Richmond, to survive. Because Gowan Pamphlet was a slave, he had no choice in the matter—he had to leave his congregation. Jane Vobe died, and David Miller, Gowan's new owner and executor of Vobe's estate, brought Gowan back to Williamsburg and his flock in 1791.

Gowan's owner drew up papers to set him free after a letter that he dropped in Yorktown brought accusations that he was a messenger for a network of armed slaves. His congregation had grown to more than 500 members by now, and as a free man he would continue to be the pastor of the only Baptist church in Williamsburg (known as the "African Church") until his death in 1807. Jesse Coles, now living in the Taliaferro House, invited Gowan's Baptist Church to hold services in his wooden carriage house on Nassau Street right down from his house. Voicing the uneasiness of Williamsburg's white population, James Semple wrote his veiled apprehension, "On Sundays and Holidays the number of Free Negroes and Mulattoes as well as slaves that is seen in the City is truly astonishing." Despite the anxiety of the white population, the "African Church" would continue to thrive; this congregation would later call itself the First Baptist Church (after the Civil War).

Ghosts Recognize the Church Has Moved to a New Building?

Although the original carriage house of Jesse Coles no longer exists, the Colonial Williamsburg exhibit of the first African church in Williamsburg has been placed across the street from the original in a stable right next to the Taliaferro-Coles House Kitchen. After Colonial Williamsburg set up the display, the ghosts seemed willing to recognize that this was the new home of the African Church. Tourists going through the exhibit have heard footsteps behind them as they walk, but when they turn around to look, there's nothing there. If tourists are loud when they walk through the stable, there is an apparition of an African American man dressed in eighteenth-century clothing that will appear to the noisy crowd and hush them. They know that it is a ghost and not a real man because he is partially transparent—and they usually get very quiet. Evidently, for the ghost, the church service is still going on, even though it's the wrong building and in the wrong century.

As for the photographic evidence, there are a number of apparitions around the building—at least four consistently appear over the exhibit. Directly in front (of the first photo) is a beautifully colored sphere. On a second visit, the lights were not on in the building, and the apparition overhead followed me over to the left side of the building. Just several feet away, in the window immediately below it, there appeared a group of apparitions that defy description, and once again the question comes up: Are there alien ghosts?

The first African American Church of Williamsburg was in a stable like this. Although this is not the original building, it seems that some congregants have accepted it as an adequate substitute. This same apparition followed me over to the left side, coming right down to the edge of the roof.

In the window immediately below the previous apparition, a strange collage of lights appeared.

Over at the church's door, a more human-like apparition partially appeared in the window.

Seconds later, the collage of lights coalesced into this alien-like image: I don't know, what would you call this apparition? It doesn't look either human or animal—some even insist alien! There are a lot of other faces in the window that are less prominent; how many do you see?

RETURN TO THE CHURCHES

Crosses, Steeples, and Lost Souls

It was inevitable that I would return to the churches—especially after the last chapter where I discovered something so bizarre in a place that was not even the site of the original church! No other places—save the Wren Building at the College of William and Mary, have as much paranormal activity as they do. (But then again, the Wren Building has a chapel inside and a small graveyard underneath!) So far, I have not come across a church—regardless of whether it's just a quarter-century or three centuries old—that does not have apparitions over it. The first question that comes to mind about all this activity over churches is why—are these former congregants who did not measure up for the rewards program in the afterlife? Or are they there as sentinels protecting the church, or guides for the living in attendance? (I have a photograph that may demonstrate that churches need protection!) Or is it just a random gathering of ghosts, perhaps buried in the area before it was developed—both Native Americans and English colonists, who are attracted to the artificial light around the outside of the building?

Another possibility that struck me is that death is just a move into another dimension; there has been some debate among physicists as to how many dimensions there are—we can only sense three at this moment in time. What if these creatures are in another dimension that exists right along side of ours, and the light that they put off bleeds over into our three dimensions. Our eyes may not be able to detect the residual light that comes from their presence, but the digital camera's sensors can. Perhaps the existence of heaven and hell, prevalent in so many religions, is not light years away, but just a dimension away—maybe a respective dimension for each.

Now if these apparitions are phenomenon that are both separate and independent of the human race, then why would they attach themselves to homes, buildings, and houses of worship? To me, that sounds illogical. Some religions want to label these creatures as demons, or spirit creatures whose only purpose is to inflict evil on the world. Would a demon be confined to one house or building, incapable of movement to another part of the world? I have captured a photo that some would label a demon, but it is the one and only time that I captured it, so perhaps it is not attached to the building where I photographed it. Wouldn't this be contradictory to their purpose (according to these very same religions) of spreading evil? That seems to be irrational, too. This project has been going on for more than four years now, and I can consistently go to certain houses, point my camera to a certain spot or window, and capture an apparition on digital media. They seem to be trapped at these locations, and incapable of moving elsewhere—although I have heard of exceptions. What I can't rationalize is why—are they there by their own volition or are they trapped or being kept there?

What makes the most sense to me is that we are creatures that have a dual existence:

As a flesh-and-blood creature, we exist as both a physical entity and as a being comprised of just energy. When we die, we are capable of living on without the physical manifestation of ourselves because our thoughts, personality, and preferences can continue on without the body, existing as pure energy. Some, upon the death of the physical body, either choose or are forced to remain attached to a place or a thing that was significant in their life as a physical being. Why else would a creature capable of intelligent thought choose to remain hovering over a house or building for years— or for who knows how long? I would be bored if it were just several days, and yet if we are to believe the ghost stories that are told, some of these creatures have been at their respective homes and buildings for several centuries! I realize that this is all speculation, and my only proof is the collection of photographs that I have—but I can't help but think about who these creatures are/were and why they show up consistently in the same place year after year.

I do want to put forth a viable and rational explanation for what I have seen based upon the thousands of digital photographs I have taken, with the caveat being that further research must be done to clarify or debunk what at this point in time appears to be a reasonable explanation.

On the next few pages, you're going to see what appears to be apparitions creating a cross over the top of Bruton Parish Church, as well as an amazing array of faces and whole figures that have appeared around this paranormal hot spot. In order to be totally objective, it's my goal in the future to check out non-Christian places of worship to discover what is going on overhead of these buildings. (I have captured one apparition hovering over a Jewish synagogue in Williamsburg.) Again I wonder why: Does it have something to do

with what's going on inside, or is it just a random thing, because as I have stated before: Are apparitions attracted to sources of artificial light? Or is it simply the fact that they died on the grounds?

The Ghosts of Christmas Past

There is an old English custom that had been in place for centuries before Charles Dickens wrote his tale of ghosts, greed, and atonement in 1843: Christmas was a time to tell ghost stories as you gathered about the fireplace— yes, Christmas was as much about ghosts as Halloween. Yet as the English tale of the paranormal and penance rose to the forefront of American Christmas culture, the English custom of telling ghost stories at Christmas took a backseat to the frantic dash to buy gifts, along with decorating the Christmas tree (a German custom introduced to America in 1842, here in Williamsburg) and the fireplace on the inside, coupled with putting up elaborate displays of lights and decorations on the outside of the home.

In an effort to resuscitate this custom, I began my search for a real ghost—once a man who when alive "communed" with the ghosts every Christmas Eve at midnight: "Tonight," he wrote in 1935, "I am in the Wythe House waiting for the hour to strike for the midnight Christmas-Eve service . . . One is not alone here. The ghosts of the past are my gladsome companions in the near midnight silence."[1] He was also a man who learned about Williamsburg's history from the ghosts. A famous newspaper columnist wrote that it was when this man "was alone, in the starlight, strolling in the night, talking with the ghosts, that he learned about Williamsburg."[2] He wrote to a ten-year-old that you can "shut your eyes and see the gladsome ghosts who once

Here is the Bruton Parish Church: Are the apparitions deliberately trying to form a cross over the church? What do you think—happenstance or a deliberate sign?

made these places their home. You can learn to call them back," he said. "You can train yourself to hear what they have to say."[3] This man was a rector of a church as well as a theologian, so the obvious question is: In death does he continue on this earth with his gladsome companions or does he go to that place of scripture, myth, and legend—depending on your belief system—where he is rewarded for living a good life?

The man was Dr. W. A. R. Goodwin, who first restored his place of worship, Williamsburg's Bruton Parish Church (built in 1715), and then took on the task of restoring the whole former capital of Virginia to its colonial splen-

dor. The quiet cleric who charmed Rockefeller out of millions to restore Williamsburg, spent many an evening in his office at the Parish House, the original home of George Wythe, a signor of the Declaration of Independence, law tutor, and friend of Thomas Jefferson, and the nation's first law professor (at the College of William and Mary). The home was built around 1750, and has been reported to be haunted for many years. (I covered the legends and lore of this house in my first book.) Evidently, Goodwin was familiar with the wraiths that haunt the Wythe House, because he wrote a woman who inquired about them, "They are very elusive ghosts and refuse to be delineated or described within the limits of any paragraph. The only way is to come here and hold communion with them." If you haven't gathered by now, ghosts were more than just metaphors

A photo of the church with the apparitions out of the
cross-shape and just hanging together.

These are three of the clearest faces that I could find
in the back windows of the Olive Branch Church.

for Goodwin—they were very real to a man who is now a ghost himself, who moved on to the realm of his gladsome companions in 1939. Goodwin knew, as I have come to find out, that *for the most part*, ghosts are not the malevolent and/or demonic variety seen in newer movies like *The Conjuring, Insidious*, and *Paranormal Activity*, or even older movies like *The Exorcist* or *The Shining*, but rather quite innocuous—and sometimes helpful.

I can't help but think that perhaps Goodwin's ghost dwells either in his former

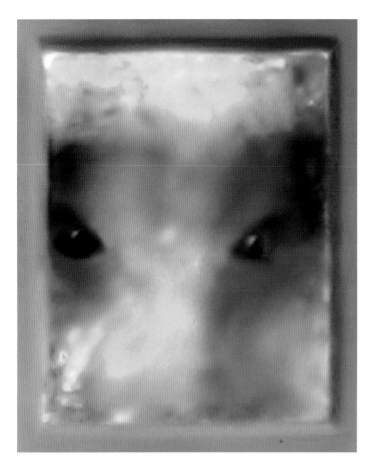

This is another example of an apparition making an appearance inside a church. Keep in mind that the Bruton Parish Church not only has distinguished members buried beneath its floors, but it also served as a temporary hospital during the Civil War—both plausible reasons for this classic-white apparition inside the sanctuary—featureless with the exception of the eyes.

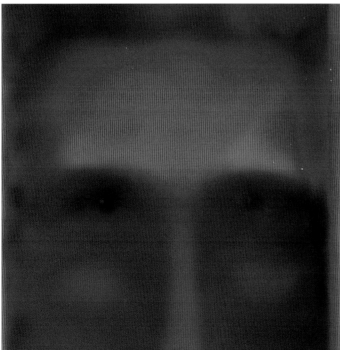

The second apparition (first in the steeple) has a different coloring, probably due to the hues given off by the candlelight; this one is the closest to a recognizable human face.

One evening we went to the Bruton Parish Church to see a friend in concert. My reluctant psychic was with me that night, and as we waited for the doors to open we sat on a bench next to the door. There was a line in the courtyard, and one woman decided to sit on a grave to wait (I blacked out her face). Picking up on the vibe, my friend leaned over and told me that a ghost was incensed that this woman was sitting on the grave. Immediately, I got up and took a photo, and you can see the streaking ghost going over to the woman. She must have been oblivious to the angry ghost, because she continued to sit on the grave until the door opened. It's something that had never crossed my mind, but I guess those souls that remain in the graveyard instead of attaching themselves to a particular house or building may get angry if their gravesite is disrespected in any way.

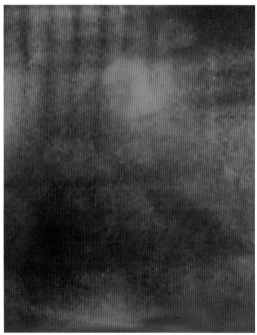

Previous apparition is enlarged and cropped to show the facial details.

Parish House or in the Bruton Parish Church, and walks the streets of the city that he helped restore. For those who would cry foul and say that the good rector has gone on to meet his maker and his reward for a life well lived, who's to say where that reward is? Perhaps it's just a dimension away from ours, and he may look in upon his former haunts (pun intended) such as the Wythe House, or he may be one of the sentinels atop the Bruton Parish Church that oversees and protects it.

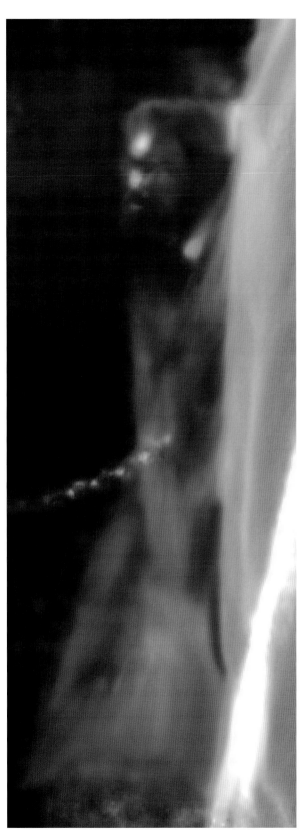

This photo has a lot going on in it. It was taken on the same night as the previous photo, and the most prominent face is a bearded man, perhaps a Confederate soldier and a victim of the Battle of Williamsburg. Strangely enough, the ghosts are about one-half the size of a normal person, and I'm thinking that the soldier is leaning in front of a woman with a long dress on (check out the partial face peering over top the soldier's head). There are a couple of other faces trying to appear—all while a group of about fifteen people wait in the church yard for a concert. Ghosts like to be around the living!

A Demon Just Outside the Church?

Bruton Parish Church holds a special place in my heart, because it was here that my paranormal odyssey began: I captured a lone apparition over the church of geometrically shaped colored light. If you would like to see that apparition and learn what it did to make such an indelible impression and inspired me to start this journey, check out Chapter 1 of my first book. It was quite a profound experience, and it was enough visual proof to make this skeptic a believer.

Since that evening, other apparitions have come out of hiding over top the church making me wonder just how many ghosts are really there. As you have already seen, one evening I even captured these apparitions forming a cross over the old church—something I have not seen since. After reading how convinced Goodwin was of the existence of ghosts, I couldn't help but think it might be him atop the old sanctuary, trying to prod me to make the rest of the world aware that Williamsburg was more than just "America's most historic avenue" (Franklin D. Roosevelt, 1934); the old colonial capitol that he knew and loved was a haven for ghosts of its historic past that are just as real as you and I.

When I was young I saw a movie that I can still recall: *The Sentinel* (released in 1977, but I'm not sure when I saw it, because I saw it some years later on television). It was a film about a blind, damned clergyman who guarded the gates to hell, innocuously disguised as a Brooklyn brownstone. I'm sure that we all would be less than impressed with the movie's special effects now, but the story was frightening. I've heard pastors talk of the malevolent spirits or demons out in the world, and this movie reminded me of that visually.

When I first saw the apparition over the Bruton Parish Church, it made me think of that lone sentinel guarding not the gates of hell, but the doorways to the church. Several years later, I was reminded what that sentinel atop the church might be guarding it from. One evening, the first night I set out on this Christmas quest, I captured an apparition on the bench just outside the doorway to the church. As I looked at the apparition, it brought back all the memories of that movie and its malevolent spirit forces. Take a look at the photo; what do you think it is? It resembles a red dragon(s), but is it a ghost? A demon? An alien? Were you as surprised as I was to see it right outside the doorway to a church? A medium I know identified the entity as a demon in wait for someone to prey upon as they exit the church—a frightening thought for anyone who attends a church, isn't it?

Here's the photo of the red dragon-like apparition that appeared on a bench right outside the Bruton Parish Church. Is this what is waiting for people just outside the entrance to their churches?

If you haven't realized from the footnotes, I have taken all of W. A. R. Goodwin's quotes from an article that the late Ivor Noël Hume wrote in the *C. W. Journal* in 2001, entitled *Dr. Goodwin's Ghosts*.[4] You see, Hume had experiences in his native England with ghosts, and as a consequence, has a visceral sense that they exist. He sought to prove his intuition by bringing a small group to the George Wythe House some years ago, hoping that the photographer who accompanied them, equipped with infrared film, might capture evidence of a paranormal presence at the old Wythe manor. Alas, he was unable to produce viable proof of the paranormal, but you can see some of the Wythe's wraiths in Chapter 8 of my first book.

After reading Hume's article online, I thought what a great Christmas odyssey to hunt not for the ghosts that haunt the Wythe House, some of which I had already found, but instead to search for the ghost of Goodwin himself. Perhaps he is in some heavenly place of unimaginable beauty light years away, or just maybe he is just a dimension away, trolling the streets at night, or perhaps hanging at the Wythe House or the Bruton Parish Church. I cannot say where he is or what he is doing, but it would be great to search for Goodwin, either in the church that he helped restore, or in the larger church of political thought called Williamsburg. In his efforts to restore the ancient capital, he often spoke of its origins in Jamestown, and how the founding fathers, such as Jefferson, Washington, and Henry, among others, discussed and debated these ideas in the homes and buildings of Williamsburg, to help form the first real democratic society in the modern world—that was his selling point to restore the capitol. Of course my selling point for Williamsburg is that not only are those ideas for democracy still here, but also some of the purveyors of that ideology still linger, and perhaps among them Rev. Dr. W. A. R. Goodwin. The search is on . . .

The Ghost Choir

The second night out on the hunt for Goodwin's ghost I discovered that there was a choral concert being held at the Bruton Parish Church. I saw a family go into the churchyard, and they stood right outside the entrance for a few minutes before entering the old house of worship, apparently not sure if they were going to attend. While they waited, I took a few photos of the area; I was worried that they might think that I was some sort of stalker— but little did they know that I had no interest in photographing them, only what was around them. What I have known for some time is that ghosts are attracted to young people, and you have already seen proof of this at the Powder Magazine when a large group of ghosts gathered around a group of middle schoolers. I have heard different theories on why this is so; perhaps the one that makes the most sense is that children have not learned to block out the sensory anomalies created by the ghosts. From my understanding, the brain gets thousands of sensory signals per second from all over the body, and must prioritize or triage these to make the conscious mind aware of only the most important. An adult's brain may discard sensory anomalies that it doesn't understand, whereas a child's brain may push through these signals to the conscious mind, making him or her aware that something supernatural is nearby.

Acutely aware of this paranormal propensity, I would later examine these photos on my computer with a great deal of interest—my visceral understanding of the supernatural would not disappoint. In one photograph I took, standing between what I assumed to be the father, his wife, and two children, was a *Phantom Choir!* While in search of the former rector, I've found a children's choir, perhaps one of Goodwin's very own during one of his two tenures as the rector of the eighteenth-century church. This group of ghostly vocalists appears to be children, perhaps four or five of them, dressed in long white robes, some with their arms outstretched as they walked—and were they singing? The irony here is that although they appear to be a choir, their mouths are missing! This mute manifestation of sacred music caught me completely by surprise; were they going into the church to watch or to participate with the living choir? My next thought was whether this choir all met their demise at the same time—or did they just get together posthumously to reform a bond they had as children. I suggest this because I've heard of a man who died of old age in another state who returned to his old Civil War regiment to participate in spying activities on the grounds of Edgewood Plantation. So where and how a person dies is not necessarily indicative of where their ghost returns to or even what they look like.

Unlike the red dragon(s) that appeared on the bench—which is straight from the camera, I had to do some work on this photo. After cropping out the family that the phantom choir stood between, I had to raise the contrast on the photo, take out the grain, and then darken in the eye detail that was lost when raising the contrast. The idea is to raise the visibility of the choir without compromising the integrity of the choir's appearance. What's evident to me from this and other photos is that humans, when they die, do not lose their desire to gather in groups with others of like mind, whether it be singing in a church choir, or marching, or even fighting together in a military "band of brothers."

Another apparent irony about the photo of this phantom choir is that these "children" may be hundreds of years old—and yet they appear forever young. Does the mind of a ghost mature on the "other side" like it matures in our dimension? In other words, though they appear as children, are they adults in their level of maturity?

Before moving on to another church, I would like to tell you the story of a paranormal sighting for which I have no photo, but the story is so compelling that I had to include it with this church. I hope to one day be able to photograph the subject of this true tale of an unlikely resident of the Bruton Parish Cemetery: Security officer Chuck Rayle happened to be at the Geddy House backyard by the fence line

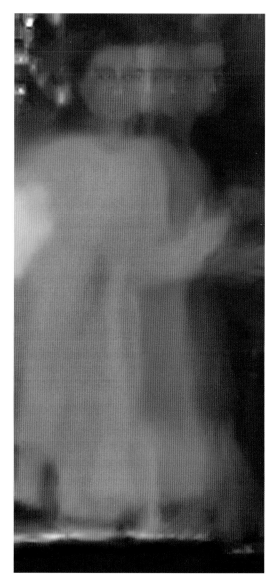

The Bruton Parish Church's Phantom Children's Choir.

on a Saturday night about 2:00 a.m. From that point, he could see three individuals: A white male, a black male, and a Hispanic male with shoulder-length hair. They stopped to look at the graveyard by the church that is visible from this location; then he observed them walk to the Carter House where they sat on the bench. Out of the corner of his eye he saw movement on his left by the Bruton Parish Church. He immediately looked to his left to see a dark figure, coming up the Duke of Gloucester Street, taking a left at the corner by the church. The figure walked on the sidewalk next to the wall of the church, and then disappeared at the tree. It happened so quickly that he had to ask himself if the figure climbed the wall by the tree to get into the cemetery. Chuck walked over and unlocked the gate to the graveyard to investigate, because the church grounds are locked at night. About halfway into the cemetery a man, about 5' 10" to 5'11" with long hair in a ponytail, wearing a tricorner hat, eighteenth-century shirt and breeches (style of pants that went from the waist to the knees), and a vest, could be seen, and yet the figure was a "construction-paper black" silhouette. He immediately realized that the dark figure was paranormal, as it disappeared into the darkest reaches of the graveyard.

Later that evening, when he informed another security officer of what he saw, she immediately asked, "Did it have an elongated neck and bulging red eyes?" After Chuck replied no, he was informed that the dark figure has been seen many times by different people, but he had just seen the rarer of the two apparitions. The most frequently seen apparition is the dark figure with the elongated neck and the bulging red eyes—an indication that the man met his end by hanging. Not only is this story puzzling because the same apparition makes an appearance both before and after he was hung, but also that there is no legacy or lore to explain the paranormal phenomena. If you are ever in

Williamsburg late at night, keep your eyes peeled for this eighteenth-century wraith—taking note of whether he appears to you in the condition before or after he was hung . . .

Not Just Bruton Parish, but All Churches and Places of Worship

Someone asked me if I was trying to frighten the congregants of Bruton Parish Church by showing the plethora of paranormal activity around it. Let me answer with an emphatic *NO*. In fact, if you go to a house of worship anywhere, of any kind, you will find ghosts there. Granted, some older churches, like Bruton, have more ghosts, not only because of the age of the sanctuary, but also because the grounds—including the inside of the church—are a cemetery. In my first book, I checked out two other churches in the area to see if the paranormal activity was comparable.

The tiny Hickory Neck Episcopal Church, a few miles outside of Williamsburg, likewise has a large cast of phantom characters for such a small building, even though church services have been moved to a newer, larger building on the grounds. I captured huge orbs over the steeple of a Baptist Church in Mathews County; some appear to be more than one hundred feet in diameter! Let me also say that I have photographed churches that are newer that have a comparable number of apparitions on the outside to that of the Bruton Parish Church; whether these were parishioners who have perished, or people who died on the grounds before the church was even built I cannot say. (Outside of Christian churches, I've gone to and photographed apparitions over a Jewish synagogue, a Unitarian Church—who accepts members of all beliefs—and an outdoor Native American ceremony.)

185

I have found multiple ghosts from the parking lot of a Williamsburg shopping center all the way to the waters of Currituck Sound; my point being that with more than one billion dead in this world, ghosts are everywhere! If you go to places like the British Isles you will find churches and buildings that are much older than Bruton Parish Church, and as a result have a longer history of hauntings. More people have died there, and consequently more of the living have had paranormal experiences and believe in ghosts. I find that like myself, most people who have not had paranormal experiences do not believe in ghosts—until they do. What will it take to make you a believer?

Giants!

You know, I thought that this would happen—the paranormal just does that to you. When you are looking for one particular presence, you find a plethora of other intriguing phantoms! I've found a red wraith that has the appearance of a dragon (or dragons—oftentimes ghosts will move so fast that their image doubles on the capture, even if the shutterspeed is only a fraction of a second, so I can't be sure if it's multiple ghosts or one caught in movement), I've found a youth choir dressed in white robes, and now I've found something equally as intriguing. I have no definitive explanations for the appearance of this ghost, but what I will offer is several possibilities for why this ghost appears as if it's a GIANT.

In my first book I took several photos of gigantic red orbs—anywhere from fifty to one hundred feet (more than thirty meters) in diameter. Two of them, one at the Mathew's Baptist Church (on page 201 of my first book you can see only one-quarter of two giant red orbs that dwarf the church steeple) and one at the Hunter Millinery (page 193 of the first book on the far right of the page, you can see the edge of a giant red orb that is at least two times the size of the one-and-one-half-story millinery) had a round shape, and the apparitions at the Wren Building at the College of William and Mary had hexagon shapes (page 99 and also on the back cover of my first book, you can see multiple red hexagon-shaped apparitions that vary in size from a basketball size to the faint outline of two orbs that are twice the size of the three-story Wren Building). It would stand to reason that if a ghost's electromagnetic field is that large, then surely it must be capable of recreating an apparition that is large—perhaps as large as the field itself—but I have never seen an overly large re-creation of a human ghost before. I use the word *re-creation* because I believe that ghosts make holograms of themselves out of light because they are now just electromagnetic fields, and they must not be able to regulate or control color, so they are usually white. So now, in the midst of my search for Dr. Goodwin's ghost, I have come across what appears to be a giant ghost. Not enormous, like some of the orbs that I spoke about, but nevertheless a giant in comparison to the surrounding real people. Whether this is a former human of a normal size who is capable of generating a much larger ghost, or an actual giant, I do not know.

Perhaps you have read or heard about a race of giants that once roamed the earth. You may have heard it through the Bible (a race of hybrid humans—the Nephilim—that were the result of what Genesis calls the "sons of God" or what some call angels, came to the earth and had sex with human women):

> There were giants in the earth in those days; and also after that, when the sons of God came in unto the daughters of men, and they bare children to them, the same became mighty men which were of old, men of renown.
>
> —Genesis 6:4

Greek mythology refers to this same group of hybrid humans as the Titans and a later group as Gigantes, along with many other references to large, humanlike monsters, like the Cyclops. I would be remiss not to mention Heracles (or Hercules), best known as the strongest of all the human/angel hybrids. Although not regarded as a giant, he was not only stronger than all of the other giants and some of their angelic or godlike fathers, but also he was the deciding factor in the victory of the "gods" over the giants.

Here in North America there are also references to fossil records of giants. The Paiute tribe, which lived in the area that is now the Southwestern states of Utah, Nevada, and Arizona, has an oral tradition of a race of red-haired, white giants that were about twelve feet tall (about four meters). They were a vicious group of cannibals that preyed on the Native American tribes in the area until they all banded together to defeat the giants. Fossil records of these beings exist in the Southwest as well as throughout North America and have been disappearing as if there is conscious effort to cover up the existence of the giants, but if you look in newspapers from the past, you can read about the recovered skeletons of giants that have since disappeared.

Whether you believe in the giants or not, you have to admit that this photo, taken in a crowd of people warming themselves around a torch set in the Governor's Green right next to Bruton Parish Church, contains the apparition of a gigantic ghost apparition in human form—the largest that I have ever photographed. If this is the ghost of a giant from the distant past or just the over-sized apparition of a perhaps bigger-than-life character from Williamsburg's past, I cannot say. The irony of the situation is that I wonder how many of these same people (or even *you* for that matter) would still be standing there warming themselves if they could see the ominous apparition looming overhead? Dare I say that the warm feeling of the fire would change to a cold chill down their spine? It's probable that some of them, regardless of the shape that they are in, would break off in a full sprint back to their cars. I have cropped the photo so that you can only see the backs of the people standing around the fire, and I blurred the face of a woman standing near me (for privacy issues).

The second photo was taken at the doorway of the Bruton Parish Church after an evening concert. I have blacked out the faces of two people leaving the church. Notice that behind them is a tall ghost, perhaps well over six feet in height.

This giant ghost appears to stand at least four to five feet higher than any of the humans warming themselves about him. The ghost is right next to the torch the people are standing around.

Could the tall ghost standing behind the two people with the blacked-out faces be the Rev. Dr. W. A. R. Goodwin? Notice that you can see his pant-leg and the shoe quite plainly (between the two people), while the rest of the ghost appears like a white mist?

If you look between the two people whose faces I blacked out, you can see that once again the shoe and the pant-leg are plain to see, but as you look to the upper body and the face, it has faded to a white, mist-like form that is not definable. (The appearance of a shoe and pant-leg with just an ephemeral mist for the rest of the ghost's body has happened before—both at the Boxwood Inn and outside the Courthouse of 1770.) The Rev. Dr. W. A. R. Goodwin was a tall man with a robust, if not athletic build—could this be Goodwin's ghost at the doorway of his church, perhaps to see off all of the guests who came to hear the evening concert? I wonder what the pressed pants with a cuff and the shoe state about the time period that this ghost lived in?

Music Attracts Ghosts

All I can think of on this particular night is that the ghosts must have had a party. Why, you ask? Because they all seem to be out! Could it be the fife and drum corps? It's quite

Here is a group of eighteenth-century ghosts on the street just outside the Bruton Parish Church. Notice the breeches and stockings to the knee on the man at the left.

possible; I've noted from several different sources, including my own experiences, that when music is playing, there is a definite draw from the other side. In other words, ghosts have an affinity for music. How do I know?

I know of an organist at the Bruton Parish Church who feels a tingling feeling on the back of the neck when practicing. Likewise I know of a piano player at the Williamsburg Inn who also gets a tingling feeling (both musicians used the word "tingling") on the back of the neck when she plays in a certain room there. (Go back to my first book for some amazing photos of some of the ghosts at the Williamsburg Inn, including a pair of ghosts that just may remind you of a Picasso painting!) I currently live in a haunted house, and I have a security camera pointed at my front entranceway that has infrared capabilities. Whenever I practice my guitar in the kitchen, I can see the monitor screen. What shows up on the screen is usually a pair of eyes—sometimes in white light and other times in black—they appear on the stairway. If there is a lot going on in the house at the time, I will sometimes see the pixilated outlines of two human-like shapes appearing and sometimes walking in the hallway or on the steps. One of the ghosts (I don't really know which one, or perhaps they both do it!) has started a new habit that rattles some of my family: He will whisper into your ear your name as if he is calling you or at least trying to get your attention, but that's all he will say. You not only hear your name being said, but you also will feel the ghost's breath in your ear and down your neck as the name is being spoken. So far, our ghosts have been quite innocuous other than that—if he (or they) decides to ramp up the activity to the poltergeist level, I will let you know . . . let's hope not.

So let's get back to the ghost party—perhaps drawn to the fife and drum music being played:

The first photo is a little blurry, but you will see amongst the ghosts shown a man who definitely lived in the eighteenth century (the 1700s) because he is wearing breeches (pants that come down to and will button just below the knee) as well as the stockings that will pull up over the knee but underneath the buttoned breeches. The women have on floor-length dresses, and the woman to the right also has a shawl over her shoulders. Someone suggested that she might be Native American—what do you think? The second photo is really a crop from the same photo—you see, there was a group of people in between the apparitions, and rather than black out all of their faces (for privacy issues), I just made two cropped photos out of the original. This is what some would call a ghost hag; the apparition was right at the wall that surrounds the Bruton Parish Church.

Can Ghosts Manipulate Light?

Are you freaked out yet? To put your mind more at ease, I think we need to go back to the hypothesis that we have an *electromagnetic consciousness*. (Please refer back to chapter 1 or in my first book starting at page 12, for a complete explanation.) If I can, let me use modern movie production as an analogy: Today we have the technology to recreate anything we can imagine on the movie screen, correct? I believe that likewise ghosts have the ability to manipulate light to recreate whatever they imagine in a hologram form, and in some cases, as in this photograph, the results are truly bizarre.

The final photo I have for you is a cropped photo taken of the sidewalk right in front of the Bruton Parish Church. This is right after the last people are leaving the church after an evening concert. Right at the entrance gate you can see the outlines of four ghosts that appeared in just one of several photos taken of the brick walkway. These apparitions, like all the people, appear to be leaving the church after the concert. I would have loved to attend

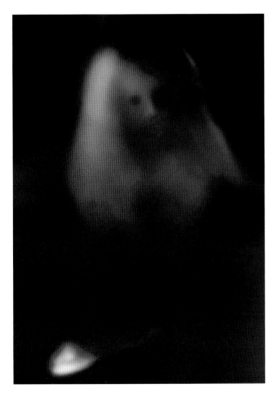

The ghost hag was near the wall that surrounds the Bruton Parish Church; note also the strange-shaped blue apparition.

Like everyone else leaving the church, these four ghosts are captured walking down the sidewalk after a Christmas concert.

this concert and just take photos of the audience. I can't tell you how many ghosts were in attendance that night, but I know there were a lot! It seemed that as I photographed people leaving the church, there were just as many ghosts streaking out the door. As it was, I was told to leave the property by someone in charge that was worried about my intentions. But if you think that this phenomenon is unique to the Bruton Parish Church, you are wrong. I have no doubt that if you attended a concert or program at your place of worship; you were in the company of ghosts!

It's Just Ghosts Passing Through . . . YOU

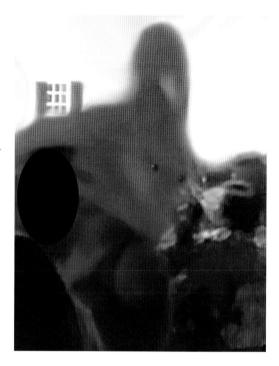

Here is a photo of at least two or more ghosts with a red/pink hue passing through a man's head (which is blacked out) as he stood in a crowd awaiting the fife-and-drum corps. The man to the right with his back to the camera has a white ghost partially covering his face.

I have felt the cold touch of a ghost that has sent icy chills from the back of my neck all the way down my spine, but I don't believe it's really "cold," even though it feels that way. If you've read my first book, you know that I believe that a hypothesis put forth by an Einstein physicist has a lot of credibility: that our souls, ghosts, spirits, or whatever you would like to call them, are intelligent, electromagnetic fields. They are pure energy, with no physical characteristics. As humans we have to consume physical things, a.k.a. food, to break down into energy to maintain our physical bodies. As a ghost you can no longer consume food, but you would still need an energy source to be active. That's why I believe that when a ghost comes near you, it draws heat energy from you—making you feel cold. Some ghosts are also able to drain batteries from cameras, EVP recording devices, and other types of ghost-hunting equipment. Whether they do this because of a need, a hunger for sustenance, or as a way to prevent you from recording evidence of their presence I cannot say, but it has

happened enough to warrant bringing extra batteries. So if and when you ever experience a "cold spot" in a room that is not coming from a physical source (for example—a poorly insulated window) then perhaps you are experiencing a ghost that is utilizing the heat energy in that area of the room to be active. I believe that a second energy source that sustains ghosts is light—which is why I believe they turn on lights in the homes they dwell in. I also have no doubt that they have learned to tap into the electrical current that runs through our homes, but I have no proof . . . yet!

According to the physicist's theory, ghosts can pass through solid objects because they are not affected by space. So if a ghost is next to you, you will probably feel a shiver down your spine (as I have) because he or she or they are absorbing your body's heat energy—

but what happens if they just pass through you? Do you still feel the cold? Have you ever felt like something has passed through you? The reason I ask is that I frequently get photographic evidence that ghosts pass through people, and I wonder what it feels like. Have they passed through me and I did not realize it? I have a photograph that illustrates what I'm saying. Of course, if I went up to the man I photographed and said to him, "I have evidence that a ghost just passed through your head. What did it feel like?"—what do you think would happen? So I keep my mouth shut and go on taking photographs; thinking that one day, with enough photographic proof, everyone will realize that the paranormal is a reality. (But then again, there are those who still believe in a flat Earth!) Take a look at the photo, keeping in mind that I had to black out the man's face for privacy reasons. Notice that the ghosts are traveling together, and it appears that they are flying just above the crowd that gathered to see the fife and drum corps, but have possibly passed right through this man's head.

The next time you are in a large crowd watching some sort of event, I can assure you that there will be ghosts among the gathering—watching and perhaps even passing through you!

Yes, the search for Goodwin's ghost continues, with each journey yielding something odd, strange, and curious. Will I find the good reverend amongst the throng of ghosts in Williamsburg, or will I keep finding things that bend and distort my (and your) reality even more?

The Ghost Cleric

I've never had trouble finding ghosts, but then again I've never set out to look for a *specific* ghost. If Dr. Goodwin's ghost would be anywhere in Colonial Williamsburg, it would be somewhere between the Bruton Parish Church and the George Wythe House, which is basically right next-door. I've stood at the main doorway to the church (through the bell tower/steeple) and photographed people as they have gone in and out of the church during evening concerts, and I have captured many apparitions this way, but none have shown enough clarity to be identified as a particular person. They have either been classic whites (a white apparition with no identifiable features—usually just two eyespots, sometimes a nose and/or mouth), or so ephemeral that, although you can make out the clothing, the facial features are so vaporous that you cannot really see what they look like. That's because when the church is in use, there is so much residual light that the apparitions are not able to compete with the brightness, and when the church is not in use, the ghosts seem to reside in an inactive state—or another dimension. Now, at other homes and buildings in Colonial Williamsburg I have been able to get clearer photos of the ghosts because the lighting is not so bright, but there are exceptions—like the George Wythe House. The Wythe House almost always has interior shutters that are drawn in the evening, and the home is almost always in total darkness—unless there is a special evening program going on at the time. So one place is too bright, and the other is too dark and closed up to capture an apparition with enough facial detail to positively identify it. So I've decided to concentrate my hunt on the walkways in between the two possible places where I might encounter W. A. R. Goodwin.

One evening between Christmas and New Years when the streets were quite active, especially on the brick walkway between Bruton and the Wythe House, I began to take photos of the area. Dr. Goodwin was an affable man who loved to be around people, so if I could not find him in the church—what better place to find the ghost of the man who *communed* (his word, not mine) with the ghosts? I took many photos that evening, and I could see some things on the review screen that were difficult to make out, but I could tell they were paranormal in nature. The review screen is too small for any detail, but when I got home and downloaded the photos to my computer, I could tell one of the photos may contain what I was searching for: It was a little blurry, but it looked like the ghost of a cleric! The ghost wore a long black robe (the same type I had seen Dr. Goodwin wear!) with a very distinct white collar—also worn by clerics of the church. Now all of the photos that I have seen of Dr. Goodwin are when he was older—bald and gray, but this photo had a younger cleric with light-brown hair—could this be Goodwin as he appeared as a young man? The ghost cleric may have a mustache (it's hard to tell—the one side appears darker than the other); I'm not sure if Goodwin had a mustache as a young man, but it is a possibility. If you look at the photo below, I don't think you will have any doubt that the ghost is a man of the cloth, and since it's on the sidewalk just outside of the Bruton Parish Church, what are the odds the ghost was a cleric at the church? But since I cannot reference any photos of a young Dr. W. A. R. Goodwin at this time, I cannot say for sure whether this man is indeed Goodwin or not. I have seen, however, a photo of an older Dr. Goodwin dressed in a long black robe just like the ghost in the photo below. (If you do a search on the Internet of images of Dr. Goodwin, you can see the same photo.) Again, keep in mind that ghosts move much faster than we do; for me this will result in distorted and incomplete photographic images—and you can see both in the lower part of the ghost's face. So I will leave it for you to decide if I have captured the elusive rector from Bruton Parish—or whether this is the ghost of another cleric from the very same church. So . . . what do you think?

The ghost cleric right outside Bruton Parish Church on the sidewalk—could this be W. A. R. Goodwin in his younger days?

BATTLE OF FORT MAGRUDER

The Fort, the Bloody Ravine, and the Killing Field

To put things in perspective, on May 5, 1862, more people died in the tiny city of Williamsburg than died in the worst terrorist attack in US history: On September 11, 2001, 2,753 people died at the World Trade Center in New York City, a city of more than eight million; on May 5, of the second year of the Civil War, 3,843 died in Williamsburg, whose residents numbered fewer than 2,000 (1,895 people, of which 743 were slaves). The rural farming community was overrun with the dead, the dying, and the wounded—numbering more than twice the population. There were not enough buildings and homes to house the wounded Confederates, who would be abandoned to the Union army as the Rebel army retreated to Richmond. Here is a little background of the battle.

The cities of Williamsburg, Yorktown, Hampton, and Newport News are all located on a peninsula, and the narrowest part is just east of Williamsburg—a bottleneck for the movement of a large army. Since June of 1861, the Confederate army used impressed slaves to dig earthen work fortifications across this narrow portion of land. The defenses, which in intervals spanned all the way across the peninsula, consisted of fourteen forts, called redoubts, made only from the ground dug up by the slaves. (By the way, this was a sore spot for the Union soldiers, who dug their own fortifications and witnessed the Southern soldiers not only using slave labor to do the most arduous tasks, but also placing slaves in the most dangerous situations while Rebel soldiers hid behind their earthen works.)

The Union had a fort at the tip of the peninsula (Fort Monroe), and the idea was to bring the Army of the Potomac down the Chesapeake Bay, land them at the fort, and quickly move up the peninsula to Richmond. They would capture the capitol of the Confederacy and promptly end the deadly Civil War. The idea may have worked if they had a bold general, but the Union commander, General George McClellan, was not that man. The advance stalled at Yorktown, and the over-cautious general, whose forces outnumbered the Confederates four to one, decided to lay a siege on Yorktown rather than attack. McClellan had 130,000 men facing off against a Confederate occupying force of 11,000—15,000; somewhere around ten to one odds.

An interesting part of the story is what General Magruder did to stall McClellan. Magruder was an actor, and he knew that he was vastly outnumbered. While he waited for reinforcements, he created a ruse that McClellan fell for: He moved troops and artillery around the ground he held to make the Union commander believe he had a lot more men than he really had—but he kept moving the same troops and equipment over and over again to make McClellan think he was moving in new troops and artillery, and that he had more than 100,000 men. The Confederate generals had already determined that the peninsula was untenable—but they needed time to dig the fortifications on the eastern side of Richmond to defend it from the Army of the Potomac. Between McClellan's fear of attack and Magruder's ability to act, the Richmond defenses were completed while McClellan waited.

On the evening of May 3, as planned, the Rebel army withdrew from Yorktown under its own artillery fire and began a retreat to the newly prepared defenses around Richmond. McClellan followed suit, and as the Union army marched up the peninsula, a rear guard was left in Williamsburg (at the line of fourteen redoubts) by Confederate General Johnston to stall the Union advance while the rest of the army marched on to Richmond. Despite a few skirmishes along the way, the Union army arrived at dawn at Fort Magruder just outside of Williamsburg and the battle began in a pouring rain that made the ground a mucky, bloody nightmare.[13]

Most of the Union soldiers were still on the road marching when the battle began; most of the Confederate army was on its way to Richmond. The battle and the rain continued throughout the day, with some Rebel units turning around and coming back to Williamsburg; the tides of battle went back and forth between the two sides. Williamsburg residents stood and watched the battle from a distance (with field glasses), and their homes were overwhelmed with the wounded and dying Confederate soldiers.[14]

Now that you know about the bloody details of the Battle of Williamsburg (Fort Magruder), it's time to look for the lost souls that still litter the battleground. I found several geo-light formations in the woods, but it seems that the ghosts in this area are prone to creating the battle sounds rather than working with light. The homes closest to these redoubts have reported hearing sounds of battle outside late at night, but are unable to see anything when they investigate. Perhaps some ghosts prefer the sound of war rather than the bloody sight . . .

On a cold winter's night, I went to the site of Fort Magruder. During the Civil War this earthen fort was described this way: "an elongated pentagon with walls fifteen feet high and nine feet thick, surrounded by a moat nine feet deep." The circumference of the fort was six hundred yards and it had eight mounted guns. Directly in front of and flanking the earthen fort was an *abatis* (a French term for a defensive obstacle of fallen trees with its branches sharpened and pointed at the enemy) of felled trees to make it as difficult as possible for the attacking Union army: As the attacking soldiers struggled to climb over the fallen trees, the South Carolina "Palmetto Sharpshooters" could pick them off. Compound that with the hard spring rain that day, and it's a wonder that the Union made any progress over the slick quagmire of mud and blood beneath the fallen trees that separated them from their objective. To make matters worse, add the artillery fire that rained down upon them, and the ground in front of this fort was a killing field.[1]

Today, only a small portion of the dirt walls remain, eroded down from their original height, strewn with trees growing out of them; the moat is filled in (probably from the eroding walls and people in the surrounding homes filling it in) and a chain link fence is around the perimeter of what's left. A road was bulldozed right through the walls; two churches, and a subdivision of houses occupy and surround the former Confederate stronghold. I wonder if any of the men who died here haunt the homes on the site of their demise (I know of several homes here that are haunted, but I do not know if the ghosts are soldiers from this battle). I found apparitions over the two streetlights just outside of the chain link fence, with several apparitions over one church and a plethora over the other; whether they are from this nineteenth-century battle I cannot say. I suspect that most of the dead would be in the area of the subdivision of homes. I did find a number of apparitions within the area surrounded by a fence, all very faint and not impressive enough to show. I also found a stacking apparition on the inside rim of the remaining part of the earthen walls that looked like a collection of possibly four or more apparitions together.

Fort Magruder
The Haunted Hotel and Cannon

The Fort Magruder Hotel and Conference Center is a distance away from the real Fort Magruder, but it is on the site of Redoubt #3, making it a hub for paranormal activity. It is very close to the Bloody Ravine (straight down Route 60), and there are a number of apparitions that I was able to photograph over the hotel. What piqued our immediate interest (I usually work alone, but I had two others with me that night) when we arrived in the parking lot was the Civil War cannon that sat on the manicured lawn in the front center of the parking area. I wrote in my first book about physicist Janus Slawinski's theory of a conscious electromagnetic field that is able to survive the death of the human body, based on two known scientific facts: that all living creatures (not just humans) emit photons of light, and that upon the death of the physical body there is a *death flash* of escaping electromagnetic radiation that can be up to one thousand times stronger than the standing emission rate. The reason I mention this is that a strong electromagnetic field can give people a headache, and as we walked to the cannon, we each got a headache that concentrated at the point right between our eyes. Thomas and a friend of his who is also

psychically sensitive both got a very strong, unwelcome message, "Back off!" as we arrived at the cannon, and felt like the crew was still working the artillery piece. When the warning did not work, our eyes began to burn, and we began to smell the smoke of burnt gunpowder—familiar to all of us—but we could not see any smoke.

My question: Are ghosts able to trick our minds into thinking that our eyes are burning and that we smell the smoke of spent gunpowder, even though it is not present? Whether real or imagined, two days later as I write this my eyes still feel like they are burning. The apparitions completely surround the cannon; unfortunately, I could not find any identifiable faces in the many photographs that I took—but we felt their presence! Besides the plethora of apparitions at the cannon, I was able to capture apparitions all over the building and parking area—some pointed at the full moon overhead and others pointed at a multitude of spotlights that illuminated the building. Employees of the hotel have spotted Confederate soldiers walking through the lobby area and exiting right through the walls of the hotel. Guests have seen a Confederate soldier in their rooms, easily recognized by his bright-red hair; some of them are completely unnerved because they are awakened out of a sound sleep when he sits on the edge of their beds. Other guests have not seen but heard the footsteps of an unseen presence walking and, in some cases, running down the hallways of the hotel. Guests and employees alike have experienced things that mysteriously disappear and reappear a little later in places that have been searched. (Some blame this playful activity not on the displaced soldiers, but on two recent additions to the hotel's paranormal occupants: a little girl who died of an asthma attack and a man who died of a stroke.) However, most of the paranormal activity at the Fort Magruder Hotel is appropriately attributed to the Civil War soldiers who lost their lives on the ground where the hotel was built.

Perhaps you too would like an authentic Civil War experience? If you stay here, be sure to take lots of photos, because the phantoms have a way of showing up where you least expect them . . .

The Killing Field

To the northeast of the amusement park Water Country, near the Colonial Parkway and the Queen's Lake subdivision, is the site where the majority of the losses were on the Confederate side. Local slaves notified Union General Keyes that two of the Confederate redoubts had been abandoned, and General Hancock and Lt. George Armstrong Custer (yes, the very same man that lost all of his men and his life to the Sioux in the Midwest) quietly marched in to occupy the Confederate redoubts.[2] When the Confederates discovered their blunder, they sent in four regiments of troops under Jubal Early to retake their fortifications. Only two regiments emerged from the tangled undergrowth to charge across a farm field, where Hancock's men mowed them down. Just as the Confederate line began to break, Hancock's men charged the Rebels and decimated the two regiments. The field was strewn with 415 Confederate dead and only seventy-five men left alive from the 5th North Carolina—and almost the same lopsided casualty count from the 24th Virginia.[3] The victorious general was given the moniker "Hancock the Superb" by the commander of the Union forces, and the field in front of Redoubt #11 would forever be haunted by the soldiers who lost their lives on that killing field.

Second Lt. George Armstrong Custer was only a twenty-two-year-old graduate of West Point when he guided Gen. Hancock's brigade across a narrow mill dam to position Union forces in abandoned Confederate Redoubt #11. After the bloody, failed assault by the 5th North Carolina and the 24th Virginia, Custer joined other Union soldiers in searching a killing field that held the lifeless bodies of so many Confederate soldiers that you could hardly take a step without treading on the dead or wounded. I doubt that he was looking for the same thing as the other Union soldiers, and what he found was a seriously wounded classmate from West Point by the name of Capt. John W. Lea. He carried his friend/foe to a nearby barn and demanded that the enemy captain be well taken care of. Lea was so grateful for Custer's care and concern that he wrote a message in Custer's notebook:

> Wmsburg, 5-6-62, If ever Lt. Custer U.S.A. should be taken prisoner, I want him treated as well as he has treated me.

Lea's recovery took weeks at the home of Williamsburg resident Col. Goodrich Durfey. This elegant home, which is still standing on the outskirts of Colonial Williamsburg, can be seen during the daylight hours by tourists, but unfortunately, I have been barred from photographing it at night—and I know that it is haunted. Margaret, the seventeen-year-old daughter of the Colonel, nursed John back to health—and the captain fell head-over-heels for his caregiver. Within two months the couple were engaged with an imminent wedding in the works. During this period the Army of the Potomac was soundly defeated during the Seven Day's Battles to the east of Richmond, and McClellan's army limped back to Fort Monroe. On the way, Custer stopped at Basset Hall to see how Lea was recuperating. The grateful couple moved their wedding up a full week so that Custer could serve as Lea's best man—the very next night. The groom and the best man wore their respective uniforms, blue and gray, side by side, with friendship superseding the ideology of the war. So congenial was Custer's reception at the Durfey home that he spent his entire two-week leave there, playing cards and listening to Southern songs courtesy of the Durfey girls. You have read about how the Civil War divided a family at the Williamsburg (Kimball) Theatre; I think it's amazing how it reunited two friends and classmates at Bassett Hall.[4] I would love to be able to photograph this eighteenth-century home just to see if I could find any of the characters in this tale looking out the windows— even Custer! I thought this was a great story to add to the legacy of carnage and sadness that was left here in Williamsburg, and I was reminded of that as I trudged through the woods in search of #11.

There is a marker for Redoubt #12 (no redoubt though), but none for #11. So using the sun as my compass, I headed east through the woods to search for the abandoned, forgotten bastion that was the site of so much bloodshed. I had to cross the Colonial Parkway, a scenic drive that connects the three points of the historic triangle: Jamestown, Williamsburg, and Yorktown. The Parkway is a concrete road with no lines, no billboards, and road signs kept to a bare minimum. After crossing the scenic road, I continued up an embankment and through the woods looking for the overgrown historical fortification. One of the things that can make a walk through the woods around Williamsburg demanding is the fallen trees: Hurricanes that come through southeastern Virginia leave their mark on the Virginia landscape by dropping huge trees, which make obstacles that can make a jaunt in the woods an arduous task.

After going around or vaulting over more than a few trees, I found the hidden historical stronghold. Like the other Civil War sites in Williamsburg, it was overgrown with trees. Hidden from the public, this redoubt was not as eroded as Fort Magruder. It still had the moat area around its base, although it had no water in it. The sides of #11 were rather steep and slick, and I needed to grasp a few saplings to climb to the top. I can imagine how much more difficult it would be for a soldier on a rainy day, carrying a gun, with no saplings or anything else to grab, and with your opponent shooting at you from the top of the wall. Once on top, I walked the perimeter of the earthen work fortification, taking photographs in the daylight, hoping to repeat my success in the Southwest by finding evidence of the paranormal while the sun was still shining. Then I climbed back down its earthen ramparts to take photos of both the walls and the area in front of the walls, which was the site of the Confederate attack. Since these photos are far less interesting and compelling, I decided to save that space for the photographs from the Bloody Ravine, perhaps one of Williamsburg's most haunted tracts of land:

The Bloody Ravine

Union General Patterson turned left off the Hampton Road going towards Williamsburg with his brigade of Union infantrymen and engaged Confederate troops in a ravine under General Wilcox. The "peninsula" is all low-lying land, and any ravines are guaranteed to be swampy areas. Couple that with the hard spring rain that was falling, and you have a recipe for a slippery, muddy mess. Now add fallen trees and undergrowth to make movement even more difficult, along with poor visibility,

Apparitions line up over the roof of the hotel as if in a military formation.

The top floor in the hotel built on the Bloody Ravine has ghosts that look out at the parking lot below, like this one. Could this be one of the African American slaves who was working for the Confederacy during this battle?

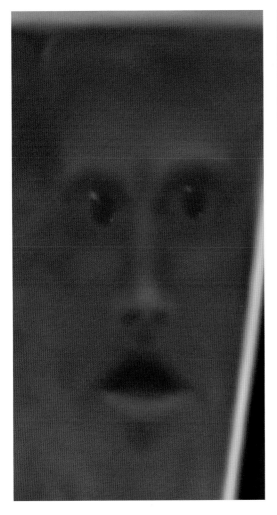

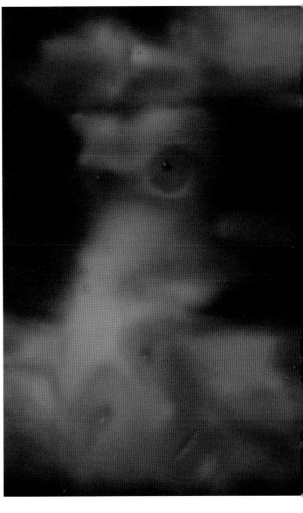

In the same room window, up to the left, is the face of fear—perhaps fear about something that was about to happen. Is this the last look on this man's face before a tragic death in the Bloody Ravine?

Across from the Bloody Ravine is an open field, and hanging out in the outskirts of the field is a number of ghosts, including this very striking stacking apparition.

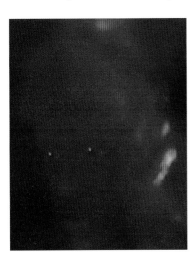

Expecting to find all soldiers, I was shocked to find among the myriad of classic whites the face of this little girl—was she an accidental victim to this raging battle or as they say in the military, "collateral damage"?

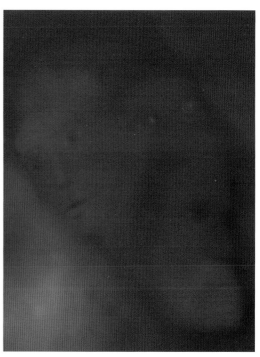

This fellow looks like he must have been in the heat of the battle; notice on the right side of his face he has what looks like an injury (blackened area)—perhaps his death-blow?

This trio was just several feet away from the first group of apparitions; just how many fought in the battle I can only imagine.

The man above was nearby; I'm not sure if he was in the battle or not, but he looks more like he belongs to Teddy Roosevelt's Rough Riders.

When I first saw this crop, it took me a minute to see that one face partially covered the much-clearer face of another possibly disembodied soldier, found under a tree down in the Bloody Ravine.

and you have the killing field that was given the moniker the "Bloody Ravine."

What started out small ended in a battle of "gigantic proportions," according to General Joseph Hooker. Patterson's men ran out of ammunition, but were backed up by Colonel Taylor's brigade of New Yorkers. Two brigades of Virginian soldiers were rushed in to support General Wilcox. All of these men on this slick hillside full of tangled growth and fallen trees resulted in hand-to-hand combat and even death by friendly fire. With the combined strength of more than a dozen regiments, the Confederates were able to push the Union advance all the way back across the Hampton Road, cheering wildly as they mounted the Union artillery. Keep in mind that not all of the Union troops had arrived yet from Yorktown, and at that moment a fresh Union brigade under General Peck appeared on the York Road and rushed in; a brigade under one-armed General Kearney appeared on the Hampton Road, and he led his men into a charge with a raised sword in his only arm and the reigns of his horse in his mouth. The Union army was able to force the Confederate soldiers back into their redoubts, with the exception of two that were left abandoned. So thus far, about mid-afternoon, everybody was back where they started—except for all of the men slaughtered in the bloody ravine—more Union troops than Confederates.[5]

Today, if you leave Colonial Williamsburg and drive down Route 60 towards the Busch Gardens amusement park, you will note that the area is very flat and level, except for one large dip in the road. You will see a railroad track on your left, and to your right you will see hotels, restaurants, and businesses—just like in any other suburban setting. At the dip in Route 60 you will notice first a restaurant (now closed) and then a hotel: The Country Inn and Suites. If you look underneath the large sign for the hotel, you will notice a rather small (in comparison to the sign) plaque in the middle of a landscaped area that sometimes gets hidden with the ornamental flowers and shrubs. Unless you look for it, you will miss it! That's all that remains to commemorate the violent battle where so many men lost their lives. What's even more disturbing is that there is no record, according to local historians, that the dead were ever removed from the temporary mass graves that were dug in the ravine. If that's the case, this is not only a battle site but also a makeshift graveyard. The parking lot on the left side of the hotel slants down at the angle, and what's left of the ravine is like it was on May 5, 1862: tangled undergrowth. But whether we want to remember them or not, the ghosts of those men who died are still there, hanging over the hotel, hanging over the streetlights in the parking lot, and hanging over the spotlights off the side of the building. They are there, sitting, standing, lying, waiting—for more than 150 years now—perhaps still in a daze about how their lives ended. Tourists drive by, go in and out of the hotel—all the while totally oblivious to the hellhole the ravine was on that one day in 1862. Tourists go to sleep in this hotel, unaware that the ghosts of Civil War soldiers are all around them—hovering over the roof, on all sides of the building, in the parking lot, at every streetlight and lamppost—watching them!

When I got to the bottom of the parking lot, I found too many hexagon-shaped apparitions to count—many were indistinguishable from each other. I would think that a city steeped in so much history would be more attentive to such a sight. Some of the most famous generals of the Civil War, from both sides, garnered their battle experience in Williamsburg. This was many soldiers' first taste of combat, particularly the Army of the Potomoc. Surely the sites of the Bloody Ravine, as well as Fort Magruder, are worth more than just a plaque—I bet the ghosts think so.

Wraiths of the Ravine

On that same frigid night in February that I went to Fort Magruder, I went to the Bloody Ravine, now the present-day site of the Country Inn and Suites, and found a lot of paranormal activity there. I discovered several apparitions over the trees in the wooded area facing south and even more apparitions over the lights of the hotel's west side. But when I went to the hotel's east side, that's when I discovered a myriad of apparitions over the lampposts in the hotel parking lot. I also captured multiple apparitions over the hotel's roof and several faces looking out of the windows on the top floor—I think most ghosts prefer the top floor because of its vantage point. Since I usually capture just the face, without any part of the lower body, I cannot say for sure if these faces are those of the men who fought in the Battle of Williamsburg. But I think given the history of this ground, there is a good chance they were among the soldiers that clashed here, whether Confederate or Union. (The majority of the casualties on this side of the battlefield were Union troops.)

For many years, soldiers from this battle have been seen in and around Williamsburg. Some have been seen running along the Duke of Gloucester Street and along Richmond Road. All of the hotels and businesses along Richmond Road (Route 60) were not present during the Civil War, and Confederate soldiers have been seen running across hotel lobbies and rooms and through the walls, still dressed in their gray uniforms, as if they were running across a field. More than 150 years later, they are still reliving the battle as if it were May 5, 1862. Some have seen wounded Confederate soldiers lying on the ground (like at the Coke-Garrett House), and others have seen them searching for missing appendages (Market Square Tavern), but the most convincing eyewitnesses have been those who live by the battlefield. Cannon fire, gunfire, sabers clashing, screams, moans, and the sounds of soldiers running, have been heard by residents there; Confederate soldiers have been seen running as if in the heat of battle, or running and hiding as if afraid of the battle. Although the Battle of Williamsburg is not considered a major battle, try telling that to the close to 4,000 casualties whose ghosts are reliving a terrible death more than 150 years later. Although I can't say the same for other areas that saw battle, the Bloody Ravine and the area to the east of it seems more than willing to show the faces of death—most are likely soldiers, but there were a few surprises in the mix. Take a look at all of the apparitions on the following pages for proof of paranormal activity that was little more than a delaying tactic by the Confederates so they could get all of their men and equipment to Richmond. Some of the Confederate soldiers are still running to Richmond, and if you come for a visit to Williamsburg and stay at one of the many hotels along Richmond Road, you may see one of them running through the lobby—or perhaps even through your room . . .

Taken at the Bloody Ravine. This photo is one of the most unique in this book: It appears to be a woman lying down at the foot of a tree. But she does not have any feet—they are actually the roots of the tree. Why would she appear with her legs and part of her right arm as tree roots? Is she part of the tree now?

WHAT I'VE LEARNED ABOUT GHOSTS

As my paranormal odyssey moves forward, I continue to observe, record, and learn. While traipsing the streets of Colonial Williamsburg at night, I have witnessed a marked increase in the security guards' activity on the nights of the full moon. I can attest to the fact that they are not finding thieves or trespassers—or they would be leading them out of the houses and buildings in handcuffs. Something is obviously setting off the motion-detector alarms in these structures— is it due to the increased activity of the ghosts? Does the full moon give them the energy to be more active during the night? I think it's a logical explanation until proven otherwise, and several security guards who work for Colonial Williamsburg endorse this explanation.

Another question I have is about a ghost's ability to recreate sights, sounds, and smells: When a ghost does this, there are usually only one or two people who experience the event. For example, the ghosts at the Raleigh Tavern recreate the sounds of a party with music and the "sweet" smell of tobacco smoke from the eighteenth century. The ghosts at the Peyton Randolph House recreate sights and sounds: the apparition of an angry man dressed in eighteenth-century clothing with the sound of heavy footsteps as well as the crashing sound of something falling or breaking glass.

My question to my readers: Since this experience usually happens to just one or two people, do the ghosts actually recreate these sensory experiences—or is it some sort of telepathic communication where just the ideas of these sensory experiences are transmitted to our brains? If they are really capable of it, why not do this in front of a large group of people? The audience is certainly available in Colonial Williamsburg . . .

Another discovery I made in this book is that although these apparitions have characteristic looks, they are capable of changing in an instant to a variety of shapes, sizes, and colors. I first ran into this metamorphosis at the William Randolph House, and I discovered an even greater array of possibilities at the Coke-Garrett House, where I witnessed a geo-light apparition go through three shape-shifts until it became this giant red hexagon that was at least thirty feet (about ten meters) high. We dress in clothing; they dress in light!

Besides the ever-morphing array of shapes and colors over haunted houses and buildings, I've also discovered a new shape that appears inside the windowpanes: the white pillar of light. Light pillars have their own set of variations that include a form without any facial features, one to two eyespots, a possible nose or nose-spot, and a possible mouth. Usually, if the form has all facial features (like the one at the jail), I will label it a "classic white." But seeing featureless white pillars, pillars with partial facial features, classic whites with a full face, and highly detailed faces that look very human—all of this begs the question: Do ghosts have to learn how to recreate their former likenesses? Don't you think that if they all could recreate their former likenesses—they all would? Are the ghosts that make a featureless white pillar just learning? Humans learn to draw, and some never learn to draw very well; does that skill set apply to ghosts too—do they learn to draw with light?

When I started this project, I thought that I should only concentrate on original eighteenth-century buildings to find the ghosts. What I discovered is that every building on the Duke of Gloucester Street and, for that matter, in

Colonial Williamsburg, regardless of whether it is original or not, has one to three apparitions over it. I thought—okay, they may not be original, but they were all reconstructed on the original foundations—maybe that's the key. What surprised me even more was that the exhibition for the first black church in Williamsburg is not even on the same piece of property! The original building is long gone, and all that is left is an empty lot, but the ghosts have moved to a new residence up and across the street. Apparitions have appeared in this new building, dressed in eighteenth-century clothing, hushing loud tourists as if church services were still going on. If it wasn't the building, the foundation, or even the original ground, what drew them to this new site?

Another strange experience that I had (as if all of this isn't strange) was to be followed around Williamsburg several times, by a phantom owl. I finally got a photograph of it, which helps to verify my story. I know the question has come up before, particularly by animal lovers, if animals have souls. I'm not here to answer that, but it would seem logical to me that an animal's ghost would do the same things in the afterlife that it did while alive. In other words, if what followed me was really the ghost of an owl, it wouldn't be following a human, but another owl, or perhaps potential prey. That's why I think that what followed me was originally human—an apparition created by a human spirit to look like the owl. I did, however, take the photo of the Taliaferro-Cole House in the first book of what looked like a white ghost of a dragonfly, seemingly frozen in flight. I will continue with an open mind and hopefully let the photographs speak for themselves, although I will tell you that the experience with the owl was more than a little creepy.

Another thing I learned about ghosts that seems rather frightening when you think about it: They are capable of starting fires. At the Cole Digges House in Yorktown, the ghost actually started a fire in the fireplace, burning the paper, kindling, and logs placed the night before by the woman who lived there. Likewise, the ghost manager of the King's Arm Tavern relights the candles in rooms where they have all been blown out. The ghosts at the Governor's Palace also play with fire, lighting candles and then blowing them out when security enters the building. It all sounds innocuous and, yes, playful when heard within the context of these three stories, but what if ghosts can set fire to buildings? Are ghosts responsible for burning down any homes or structures?

Let me start my last observation with a question: Do some (or all) ghosts have this incredible ability to master technology they've never used? I ask this question based on two experiences: One, my own experience in front of the Dean House and a documented experience of a William and Mary student doing a film project in the haunted Tucker Hall. The first was with a ghost that got inside of an iPhone that my sister was using to take a photo of the Elkanah Dean House. As she aimed the iPhone at the house, all you could see in the viewfinder was the face of a man in black and white. He was actually smiling as if posing for the picture. How was the ghost able to figure out how to get its image inside the camera? The second experience involved two William and Mary students converting and burning a film to DVD. The ghost was able to insert photos of classmates' faces, as well as random film footage from the Internet, onto a DVD—right after they had checked their film file to make sure it was precisely what they had created. The computer technology that they used was not even in existence when this ghost passed on, yet it was able to master the technology as well as navigate the Internet to change the film. How? Are they able to master it on their own, or do they access our thoughts to learn?

Are they capable of mastering technology in just a few seconds the way that ghost accessed the iPhone? What kind of an IQ do they have to be able to do that?

My journey continues as I try to both find and develop new and better technology to eliminate all doubt that the paranormal world exists. Who knows, I may even find proof of the existence of other dimensions! I also plan to write a book explaining all the details of how I photograph the paranormal, so that if you so desire, you can go out and get the same kind of results that I've discovered. So until then, stay tuned!

Finally I would like to mention a trip to the Southwest, because it was there that I found that the saga continues—even during the daylight hours when I was not looking for ghosts—but they, and some other strange phenomena, found me. My point is that the paranormal is not just in Williamsburg, but everywhere, and I hope to share these photos that were taken in the broad daylight out in the Southwest soon, as there is not room in this book. As I continue to photograph and discover things about a world that for many years I did not believe existed, I find that it is amazing, diverse, and capable of stretching one's imagination past our limits of comprehension—more so than some of the finest creative minds in the motion picture industry. I hope the photos in this book have given you a glance into this netherworld of death and that they may find you redefining your perception of human mortality—or should I say immortality? I likewise hope that the technology improves to such a degree that even the naysayers have to admit they're wrong. (To that extent, I have ideas about ways to improve the camera's ability to capture this world, but that is going to take more time and money.) Till then, know that your eyes do not reveal everything that is in our world—you may think you're alone, but YOU'RE NOT!

ENDNOTES

1. Slawinski, Janusz, "Electromagnetic Radiation and the Afterlife, New Dualism Archive," 1987 (Accessed March 25, 2015), PDF document available online: www.newdualism.org.

2. McFadden, Johnjoe, "Our Conscious Mind Could Be an Electromagnetic Field," UniSci. May 16, 2002 http://unisci.com/stories/20022/0516026.htm (Accessed January 14, 2016).

3. Independence Hall Association, "General Anthony Wayne," 2006–2015, www.ushistory.org/paoli/history/wayne.htm (Accessed December 30, 2015).

4. Independence Hall Association, "General Anthony Wayne," 2006–2015, www.ushistory.org/paoli/history/wayne.htm (Accessed December 30, 2015).

5. Civil War Trust, "The Battle of Williamsburg, 2014," www.civilwar.org/battlefields/williamsburg.html (Accessed September 22, 2014).

6. Yetter, George Humphrey, "When Blackbeard Scourged the Seas," *Colonial Williamsburg Journal,* Vol. 15, (Autumn 1992), pp. 22–28. No. 1, www.history.org/Foundation/journal/blackbea.cfm (Accessed February 15, 2015).

7. Gill, Harold Jr., "Williamsburg and the Demimonde: Disorderly Houses, the Blue Bell, and Certain Hints of Harlotry," *CW Journal,* Autumn 2001, www.history.org/foundation/journal/autumn01/demimonde.cfm (Accessed October 17, 2015).

8. Fredericks, Erica, "Evidence of a Ghostly Encounter at Tucker Hall?" *Arts and Sciences 2001–06 Archive,* March 6, 2006, www.wm.edu/as/english/news/2001-06/evidence-of-a-ghostly-encounter-in-tucker.php (Accessed 01/17/2015).

9. Hume, Ivor Noel, "Doctor Goodwin's Ghosts, A Tale of Midnight and Wythe House Mysteries," *CW Journal,* Spring 2001, www.history.org/foundation/journal/spring01/wythe_ghosts.cfm (Accessed 03/04/2017).

10. Tobias, Herbert Ezekiel, *The Recollections of a Virginia Newspaper Man*, March 22, 2010 (Charleston, SC: Nabu Press).

11. Hume, Ivor Noel, "Doctor Goodwin's Ghosts, A Tale of Midnight and Wythe House Mysteries," *CW Journal,* Spring 2001, www.history.org/foundation/journal/spring01/wythe_ghosts.cfm (Accessed 03/04/2017).

12. Hume, Ivor Noel, "Doctor Goodwin's Ghosts, A Tale of Midnight and Wythe House Mysteries," *CW Journal,* Spring 2001, www.history.org/foundation/journal/spring01/wythe_ghosts.cfm (Accessed 03/04/2017).

13. Civil War Trust, "The Battle of Williamsburg, 2014," www.civilwar.org/battlefields/williamsburg.html (Accessed September 22, 2014).

14. Gruber, D. A. "The Battle of Williamsburg, 2014," October 30, *Encyclopedia Virginia*. www.EncyclopediaVirginia.org/Williamsburg_The_Battle_of (Accessed September 22, 2014).

15. Civil War Trust, "The Battle of Williamsburg, 2014," www.civilwar.org/battlefields/williamsburg.html (Accessed September 22, 2014).

16. Civil War Trust, The Battle of Williamsburg, 2014, www.civilwar.org/battlefields/williamsburg.html (Accessed September 22, 2014)

17. Erickson, Mark St. John, "A Union Hero Shows His Mettle in the Battle of Williamsburg, July 22, 2013," *Daily Press*, www.dailypress.com/features/history/our-story/dp-battle-of-williamsburg-20130722-post.html (Accessed September 22, 2014)

18. Erickson, Mark St. John, "Custer Finds a Confederate Classmate among Williamsburg's Civil War Wounded, August 12, 2013," *Daily Press*, www.dailypress.com/features/history/civilwar/dp-custer-confederate-classmate-battle-of-williamsburg-20130812-post.html (Accessed September 23, 2014).

19. Civil War Trust, "The Battle of Williamsburg, 2014," www.civilwar.org/battlefields/williamsburg.html (Accessed September 22, 2014).

BIBLIOGRAPHY

All of the historical information for the buildings in Colonial Williamsburg was taken from the following two sources:

Colonial Williamsburg's website: www.history.org/.

Olmart, Michael, Suzanne E. Coffman, and Paul Aron. *Official Guide to Colonial Williamsburg, Third Edition.* Williamsburg, VA: Colonial Williamsburg Foundation, 2007.

Additional Sources

Barefoot, Daniel W. *Spirits of '76: Ghost Stories of the American Revolution.* Winston-Salem, NC: John F. Blair. 2009. p 237.

Civil War Trust. "The Battle of Williamsburg, 2014." www.civilwar.org/battlefields/williamsburg.html (Accessed September 22, 2014).

Erickson, Mark St. John. "A Union Hero Shows His Mettle in the Battle of Williamsburg." July 22, 2013. *Daily Press,* www.dailypress.com/features/history/our-story/dp-battle-of-williamsburg-20130722-post.html (Accessed September 22, 2014).

Erickson, Mark St. John. "Custer Finds a Confederate Classmate among Williamsburg's Civil War Wounded." August 12, 2013. *Daily Press,* www.dailypress.com/features/history/civilwar/dp-custer-confederate-classmate-battle-of-williamsburg-20130812-post.html (Accessed September 23, 2014).

Fredericks, Erica. "Evidence of a Ghostly Encounter at Tucker Hall?" *Arts and Sciences 2001–06 Archive.* March 6, 2006. www.wm.edu/as/english/news/2001-06/evidence-of-a-ghostly-encounter-in-tucker.php (Accessed January 17, 2015).

Gill, Harold Jr. "Williamsburg and the Demimonde: Disorderly Houses, the Blue Bell, and Certain Hints of Harlotry." *CW Journal.* Autumn 2001. www.history.org/foundation/journal/autumn01/demimonde.cfm (Accessed October 17, 2015).

Gruber, D. A. "The Battle of Williamsburg, 2014." October 30. *Encyclopedia Virginia.* www.EncyclopediaVirginia.org/Williamsburg_The_Battle_of. (Accessed September 22, 2014).

Hume, Ivor Noel. "Doctor Goodwin's Ghosts, A Tale of Midnight and Wythe House Mysteries." *CW Journal,* Spring 2001. www.history.org/foundation/journal/spring01/wythe_ghosts.cfm (Accessed 03/04/2017).

Independence Hall Association. "General Anthony Wayne." 2006–2015. www.ushistory.org/paoli/history/wayne.htm (Accessed December 30, 2015).

Independence Hall Association. "Wayne Buried in Two Places." 2006–2015. www.ushistory.org/paoli/history/wayneburied.htm (Accessed December 30, 2015).

McFadden, Johnjoe. "Our Conscious Mind Could Be an Electromagnetic Field." *UniSci.* May 16, 2002. http://unisci.com/stories/20022/0516026.htm (Accessed Jan. 14, 2016).

Pockett, Susan. "Field Theories of Consciousness." *Scholarpedia.* 2013. www.scholarpedia.org/article/Field_theories_of_consciousness (Accessed January 14, 2016).

Slawinski, Janusz. "Electromagnetic Radiation and the Afterlife, New Dualism Archive." (1987, accessed March 25, 2015), PDF document available online:wwww.newdualism.org.

Tobias, Herbert Ezekiel, *The Recollections of a Virginia Newspaper Man.* Charleston, SC: Nabu Press, 2010.

Yetter, George Humphrey. "When Blackbeard Scourged the Seas." *Colonial Williamsburg Journal,* Vol. 15. Autumn 1992. pp. 22-28. No. 1. www.history.org/Foundation/journal/blackbea.cfm (Accessed February 15, 2015).